ALESSANDRO SCARLATTI

Alessandro Scarlatti

AN INTRODUCTION
TO HIS OPERAS

DONALD JAY GROUT

University
of California Press

Berkeley, Los Angeles, London

University of California Press
Berkeley and Los Angeles, California

University of California Press, Ltd.
London, England

Copyright © 1979 by
The Regents of the University of California

ISBN 0-520-03682-4
Library of Congress Catalog
Card Number: 78-54796
Printed in the United States of America

1   2   3   4   5   6   7   8   9

ƐⲂ
Ⲥᗞ

The Ernest Bloch Professorship
of Music and the Ernest Bloch Lectures
were established at the University of California
in 1962 in order to bring distinguished figures
in music to the Berkeley campus from time to time.
Made possible by the Jacob and Rosa Stern
Musical Fund, the professorship was founded
in memory of Ernest Bloch (1880–1959),
Professor of Music at Berkeley
from 1940 to 1959.

THE ERNEST BLOCH PROFESSORS

1964   RALPH KIRKPATRICK
1965–66   WINTON DEAN
1966–67   ROGER SESSIONS
1968–69   GERALD ABRAHAM
1971   LEONARD B. MEYER
1972   EDWARD T. CONE
1975–76   DONALD JAY GROUT
1976–77   CHARLES ROSEN
1977–78   ALAN TYSON

CONTENTS

·I·

The *dramma per musica*
in Scarlatti's Time

For every hundred people who know about, or who at least have heard, the music of Domenico Scarlatti I suppose there are perhaps three or four who know about or have heard much of the music of Domenico's father, Alessandro. Of course, fathers on the whole are not a very highly regarded species in present-day society, but there are a number of other good reasons for this ignorance about Alessandro Scarlatti. For one thing, he had the misfortune to live and work in a period that is not very fashionable in the currently orthodox music-historical thinking: he belongs to the generation just before those great figures of the late baroque, J. S. Bach, Handel, Rameau, and Vivaldi. Scarlatti's productions span the forty-five years from 1680 to 1725. In the latter year, that of Alessandro Scarlatti's death at the age of sixty-five, Bach and Handel were forty years old. Bach had just entered on his post at Leipzig; he had already produced the *Orgelbüchlein,* the *Brandenburg Concertos,* the Clavier Suites, the first volume of the *Well-Tempered Clavier,* and many cantatas; but the *St. Matthew Passion,* the later chorale preludes, the B-Minor Mass, the *Goldberg Variations,* the *Musical Offering,* and *The Art of Fugue* were still in the future. By 1725 Handel was well launched at London on his career as an opera composer and impresario, but many of his operas and all the great oratorios were still to come. Rameau had published his famous treatise on harmony, and a few harpsichord pieces, but was as yet practically unknown as a composer; the first of his operas, *Hippolyte et Aricie,* dates from 1733. Vivaldi in 1725 was busily writing operas, oratorios, concertos, and cantatas and conducting concerts at Venice, with nearly half of the productive years of his life still before him.

These four contemporaries seem to tower across the landscape of musical history like a range of mountains, casting a huge shadow behind them—a shadow that stretches in our music-historical imagination all the way back to Monteverdi. In that shadow lies the work not only of Alessandro Scarlatti but also of Carissimi, Cavalli, Cesti, Lully, Corelli, Legrenzi, even Purcell—all composers known well by a few specialists, fairly well by general music historians, and temporarily by students in music history courses. There are two categories of composers in the history of music who deserve commiseration from all right-thinking people: those unfortunates who are commonly lumped together under the heading either of "followers" or "predecessors," and therefore in either case condemned to perpetual obscurity. Alessandro Scarlatti is not in any important sense either a follower or a predecessor of anyone in particular, but the fact remains that his reputation has always suffered from the historical bad luck of his having been born just twenty-five years before Bach and Handel.

Historical bad luck, however, does not wholly account for the neglect of this composer. Scarlatti wrote in all the large musical forms of his day, but the great bulk of his work, and certainly the most important part of it from any standpoint, is vocal. His keyboard pieces and his sonatas and concertos, while far from negligible, are not outstanding in an age adorned by the productions of such masters as Couperin, Corelli, Torelli, Kuhnau, and Georg Muffat. The oratorios, on the other hand, include some of Scarlatti's best work, and are now receiving long overdue recognition.[1] Also among his sacred vocal works are ten masses, some in the traditional "Palestrina" style and others in the new "concertizing" style for soloists, chorus, and full orchestra. Deserving of special mention is the *Passion according to St. John,* that austere and extraordinarily moving work written at Rome when Scarlatti was only nineteen years old.

Overtopping all the instrumental and all the sacred vocal works, however, in both amount and importance, are Scarlatti's

1. Modern ed. by Lino Bianchi (Rome: De Santis, 1964–).

cantatas and his operas. There are some eight hundred cantatas, most of them for solo voice and basso continuo, dating from every period of the composer's life. Scarlatti scholarship will always be indebted for the basic bibliographical study of this vast treasure of music to Edwin Hanley.[2] We may hope that sometime before Western civilization collapses, an editor, or a team of editors, will undertake the publication of the cantatas, or at least a large enough selection of them to enable us to appreciate more justly the full scope of Scarlatti's achievement in this genre. He was the last great master to devote so much of his energy to the Italian cantata, crowning the work of Carissimi, Rossi, Stradella, and others of the seventeenth century. Putting aside (if we may do so for a moment) all such mundane considerations as costs of publication, sales, subsidies, and the like, there seems to be no reason why we should not be as much entitled to have a collected edition of Scarlatti's 800 cantatas as two Gesamtausgaben of Schubert's 600 lieder.

As for Scarlatti's operas, the bibliographical situation is less satisfactory than in the case of the cantatas. On the title page of the autograph score of *Griselda* (1721) it is stated that this is the composer's 114th opera. If Scarlatti did indeed write 114 operas, as he appears to claim, it seems that fully half of them have utterly disappeared and that about half of the remainder survive only in what are called fragments—anything from a couple of isolated arias in miscellaneous collections to a score like that of *Eraclea* which contains all the arias but hardly any of the recitatives. Still, there remain some thirty or thirty-five operas that are salvageable, and it may be hoped that these, or at least a good part of them, will eventually appear in the collected edition now under way at the Harvard University Press.[3]

Because the importance of Alessandro Scarlatti (like that of the majority of composers of his time) arises chiefly from vocal

2. Edwin Hanley, "Alessandro Scarlatti's *Cantate da Camera:* A Bibliographical Study" (Ph.D. diss., Yale University, 1963).

3. Alessandro Scarlatti, *The Operas of Alessandro Scarlatti,* ed. Donald J. Grout (Cambridge: Harvard University Press, 1974–); vol. 1, *Eraclea* (1974); vol. 2, *Marco Attilio Regolo,* ed. Jocelyn Godwin (1975); vol. 3, *Griselda* (1975); vol. 4, *La principessa fedele* (1977); vol. 5, *Massimo Puppieno,* ed. H. Colin Slim; vol. 6, *La caduta de' decemviri,* ed. Hermine Williams; others forthcoming.

works, his reputation is peculiarly subject to the depredations of time. Such is always the case with vocal music from a historical period, which, like that in which Scarlatti lived, is separated from our age not merely by the passage of years but also by those drastic changes in musical style that resulted from historical events of the later eighteenth century—changes in the structure of society, in aesthetic theory, in the organization of musical life and the conditions of musical performance, changes whose results, by and large, are still with us to this day (even though by now beginning to be considerably eroded). The old saying that music is a "universal language" has some validity when applied to instrumental music, but hardly any when applied to vocal music. Scarlatti's orchestral works can be and occasionally are still heard in concerts; that is to say, they can be played at the kinds of occasions on which we now customarily listen to music. This is not so of his vocal works. His masses and oratorios were written on demand for specific occasions in certain churches or chapels. The cantatas were produced likewise for specific occasions—meetings of academies, gatherings of friends in the household of a patron, or the like; and the operas similarly for a particular theatre or palace, for particular singers, and for the customary occasions in the musical life of the time at Rome, Naples, Florence, Venice, or elsewhere. The oratorios were seldom repeated, the cantatas practically never. The operas were repeated for one or two seasons at most, and if they were later taken up at other cities it was always with additions and changes to adapt them to particular local demands. The life of the average opera in early-eighteenth-century Italy was about as long as that of the average pop song in America today. There was constant demand in that age for music, but it was always for new music. Nowadays we hardly ever hear an oratorio in church and only seldom in a concert hall (and then it is apt to be either *Messiah* or *Elijah*). Household music, except for the kind that comes out of loudspeakers, is a thing of the past. And as for opera, it survives precariously, by the help of private and public patronage combined with mass appeal, having a repertoire made up almost wholly of old favorites repeated season after season. One can easily imagine a Scarlatti oratorio occasionally being sung today in church or in concert or a cantata as one item in a song recital, but it is more difficult (though perhaps not quite impossible) to imagine a Scarlatti opera being staged at a modern opera house.

At this point it may be asked, if vocal music of past epochs is so especially liable to the ravages of time, how does one account for the evident continuing vitality of Palestrina or the current interest in the music of Josquin and that of the Renaissance madrigalists? And then what about the vocal works of Bach, Handel, and Rameau which, like those of Scarlatti even if a little later, still come from the prerevolutionary first half of the eighteenth century? One possible answer lies in the idea of "shelters": Palestrina's music survived for a long time (like Gregorian chant) under the shelter of the church; that of Josquin and the Renaissance madrigalists, after nearly three centuries of relative obscurity, is flourishing today under the shelter of the universities, the learned societies, or groups of cultivated amateurs, whence it radiates outward to a somewhat limited general musical public. Handel's oratorios have had an unbroken line of public performances; his operas, like those of Rameau, Monteverdi, and Cavalli, are now again becoming known through the efforts of circles of admirers who, working largely from under the academic shelters, have succeeded in pushing them a little way into public consciousness. Vivaldi's operas, like those of a great many other eighteenth-century composers before Mozart, still await promotion. Bach's vocal works have been universally admired for a century and a half; they can be sung practically anywhere, they require no staging, and their texts are such as do not obviously need complicated explanations for the benefit of uneducated listeners. Perhaps fortunately for his later reputation, Bach did not write operas.

For it is opera, of all the forms of music in our Western world, that is most vulnerable to changes wrought by the passage of the years: first, because it always involves a huge investment of work, time, and money to produce; and second, because it is inseparably bound up with texts that assume a body of unconsciously held beliefs and attitudes many of which are foreign to our ways of thinking today and hence require an effort of historical imagination to appreciate. Furthermore, Italian operas of the early eighteenth century embody certain techniques of performance that

are no longer part of our common musical background or education, such as the impromptu realization of figured basses and
especially the more or less elaborate improvised (or ostensibly improvised) ornamentation of the vocal melody in arias. Their conventions of stage scenery and costume, of dramatic subject matter,
of poetic form and poetic language, and of musical form in both
broad and detailed aspects are all part of a musico-dramatic world
that is perfectly consistent within itself, perfectly consonant with
the social conditions of its time and place, but remote—in some
ways terribly remote—from the world in which we live today.
Remote—but not unattainable. I believe it is worthwhile to try to
attain an understanding of that world, to enter as far as we can
into that portion of our musical heritage. Scarlatti's operas can still
be heard with pleasure. To comprehend them, both as an aesthetic experience and as the reflection of a particular place and
time in our common history, is an aim not unworthy of an educated person today. Historically these works may be said to mark
the culmination of the first hundred years of Italian opera. They
represent a certain ideal form of musical drama that was widely
prevalent in the late seventeenth and early eighteenth centuries,
one that differs in many ways from the ideal forms of later
masters—Mozart, Wagner, or Debussy, for example—in ways that
are interesting because all these diverse kinds of opera share one
common end and purpose: that of expanding the dimensions of
our awareness of the world and of the potentialities of human
achievement. The desire to comprehend such matters is something that sets us human beings apart from the rest of the animal
kingdom; and it is one sign of our human status that we will
undertake to satisfy such a desire not because we have to but simply because we want to.

The best way to become acquainted with Scarlatti's operas is to
start where the composer himself started, namely with the librett-
tos. Unless an opera composer writes his own librettos (as Wagner
did) he enters upon his work confronted by a *fait accompli* in the
shape of a text prepared by someone else, a drama on a subject
calculated to appeal to the interests of a prospective audience and
in a form corresponding more or less to that audience's expecta-

tions. The unexpected, the element of surprise, entered the calculations of Scarlatti's librettists only with regard to details—and then not to "corroborative detail intended to give verisimilitude to an otherwise bald and unconvincing narrative," as Pooh-Bah would have expressed it, because verisimilitude was the last thing a seventeenth-century librettist worried about, but only with regard to what may be called conventional ornamental detail. Apart from such detail, there is a very marked uniformity in both subject matter and treatment among Scarlatti's operas. The great majority are of the kind called *dramma per musica*, that is, a drama with or for or by means of music. They are laid out practically always in three acts. Their subject matter comes from ancient (sometimes medieval) history, or from legends believed or half-believed to be historical: witness such titles as *Pompeo, Flavio, Massimo Puppieno, La caduta de' decemviri, Tito Sempronio Gracco, Il gran Tamerlano, Marco Attilio Regolo,* and many similar. Other serious subjects are adapted occasionally from literary sources, for example *Griselda* from Boccaccio; still others (like *La principessa fedele*) are apparently free inventions of the poets. In addition to serious dramas of this sort there are two other classes of subjects: the comedies, sometimes called *commedie in musica,* that is, straight dramas in a light mood, not necessarily comic in the sense of farcical; and the pastorales or pastoral-comedies, these mostly from Scarlatti's early years.

But elements of the pastorale and of comedy in both senses of the word are common ingredients within the serious dramas too. Nearly always in these works there will be at least one pastoral episode with a background of supposedly "wild" natural scenery. (Incidentally, this kind of setting appears to have had strongly soporific properties, to which ladies were peculiarly subject: Statira, in the opera of that name, even manages to sleep through an earthquake.) Even more conspicuous than the pastoral episodes, however, are the comic scenes in Scarlatti's serious operas. These always come at certain definite spots: at the end of Acts I and II, usually also toward the end of Act III. They are clearly defined units, contrasting sharply with the rest of the opera not only in mood but also in the style of the text, the melodic style, and the orchestration. It is easy to see that it would be only a matter of time—in fact, the process was beginning already in Scarlatti's lifetime—before such comic scenes would become formally detached from a serious opera and begin to flourish on their own as "intermezzi," like the famous *Serva padrona* of Pergolesi which began life as a pair of comic interludes between the acts of his serious opera *Il prigioner superbo* at Naples in 1733.

The personages whose antics furnished material for the plots of Scarlatti's *drammi per musica* represented three distinct social classes: (1) rulers—kings, princes, generals, chieftains—always shown as wielding despotic power over everyone else in the cast, invariably brave and imperious, passionately dedicated to maintaining their own "glory" and preternaturally sensitive on the subject of "honor," but capable of the most exemplary tender affection toward their own wives, mistresses, and eventual children, or at least toward one attractive lady whom they sought (usually) in honorable marriage; (2) courtiers, ministers, and confidants, male or female, all belonging to what may be called the middle noble status, some of them loyal to their ruler, some treacherous, as might be required for the weaving of the plot; and (3) servants, who in turn are of two separate classes: (a) attendants, usually faithful and devoted to their immediate superiors and (b) at the bottom of this social ladder a pair of servants, typically a man (usually a bass) and a woman or boy, who appear only sporadically in the serious portions of the opera but who always have the comic scenes wholly to themselves. The function of these scenes with respect to the whole piece is similar to that of the satyr play in Greek drama or the "buffo" or "clown" scenes in Shakespeare.

Within the groups of the serious characters there will always be at least two pairs of lovers; the comic servants will make still a third pair, and in their case the comedy may sometimes be accentuated when the "female" partner turns out to be a man or boy in disguise. Disguises, of course, are an indispensable feature of these operas: without them, the whole plot would fall to pieces before it ever got started; and they are always perfectly impenetrable. So far as I know, no one in any of these operas ever has even the remotest suspicion that a disguised character is anyone other than he is pretending to be, until the moment comes when his true identity has to be revealed.

The protagonists are thus, as it were, stylized persons: not persons with all their individual idiosyncrasies, but rather types, representatives of certain stations in the social order, displaying the qualities and traits proper to those stations. Their world is not a picture of the actual world in which people then lived, but rather a diagram of it, a diagram deliberately simplified to show certain essential relations but not aiming or pretending to depict concrete reality. This abstract, diagrammatic quality of the background is in one way covered and in another way accentuated by the nature of the motives that supposedly actuate the characters. Chiefly it is love that makes the world of these dramas go round. Their action swirls about the various love affairs with all their attendant pains, perils, deceptions, jealousies, and misunderstandings until the inevitable *lieto fine* or "happy ending," where all the couples are finally sorted out and launched on a life which presumably will continue happily ever after. This consummation is usually brought about not by luck, still less by any intelligent planning by the persons chiefly concerned, but rather by the last-minute intervention of the ruler, in an exemplary act of renunciation inspired by pity and greatness of soul. The well-known figure of the "magnanimous tyrant" in these dramas is not an arbitrary or merely fashionable convention; it is a symbol. The king, in the social hierarchy of Scarlatti's time, was the secular representative of God. It was in high conformity to that divine model that he should be represented as displaying his mighty power chiefly in the showing of mercy and pity. Incidentally, it is possible (though I have not the statistics to prove it) that the magnanimous tyrant appeared on the stage more often in the kingdom of Naples than in some other Italian cities. For example, the original libretto of *La principessa fedele* for Venice in 1709 had a tyrant, to be sure, but he did not appear at all in the last scene of the opera. When the libretto was adapted for Scarlatti at Naples in the following year, however, a whole new final scene was added, for no other purpose (apparently) than to represent the sultan of Egypt as a benevolent despot, prepared at last to make an honest woman of his favorite concubine, releasing his two slaves, the young hero and heroine, from captivity, swearing eternal friendship with the empire, and in general making everything right for everybody—and all this freely, of his own magnanimous will, with no external constraint whatsoever.

The formal framework within which the plots evolve is quite uniform (not to say rigid) throughout Scarlatti's operas and indeed generally in all Italian operas of his time. These works consist of a series of distinct scenes, in number anywhere from a dozen to eighteen or twenty in each of the three acts: and the internal structure of each scene and the principles which govern the succession of scenes within one act are subject to certain general rules of construction. In order to understand this framework it is necessary first to have clearly in mind what is meant by a scene in these operas. Unlike its usual modern sense, the word *scene* in Italian operas (as indeed generally in all dramas of the Scarlatti period) does not necessarily imply a change of place— that is, a change of stage set. A new scene begins, in principle, whenever a personage enters or leaves the stage, so that a whole series of three, four, or more scenes (in this technical sense) may be played against the same background of décor. Changes of stage setting do, of course, occur; there may be two, three, or even four such changes within each act. They will be planned in such a way as to assure variety and contrast, and will be as varied and magnificent as the resources of the theatre or the amount of money available for a given production permit. Among the more elaborate settings are throne rooms, public squares, military encampments, and other places suitable to the rank and dignity of the great personages, such backgrounds usually involving crowds, ceremonial processions, triumphal entries, or disembarkations, sometimes with ballets (but seldom choruses). In 1696 the viceroy at Naples greatly enlarged the Teatro San Bartolomeo in order to make room for bigger and better stage facilities; on the whole, however, the stage settings of Scarlatti's operas, whether at Naples or Rome, do not seem to have been so elaborate and costly as those of many Venetian operas of the seventeenth century, with their celebrated machines and spectacular stage effects.

Now to return to the structure of a scene in the precise sense which the word invariably has in the librettos and scores of Scarlatti's operas. A scene may consist of two elements: dialogue, which carries on the action; and monologue, in which a given personage or group of personages confides to the audience his or her or their opinions and sentiments in the face of the situation at a certain point in the action. The two terms must be more particularly defined. A "dialogue" does not necessarily involve two or more persons present on stage: it may be internal. One person alone may be holding as it were a conversation with himself, or settling within his own mind just what the present situation actually is or what it involves in his own case. Likewise a "monologue" may sometimes be uttered by two, three, or four persons at once, all expressing identical or at least closely similar opinions and sentiments arising out of a given situation. The essential difference is that dialogues are addressed to someone on the stage, whereas monologues are addressed to the audience. By analogy with ancient Greek drama, dialogue corresponds to the speeches of the actors, monologue to the choruses. Both dialogues and monologues are usually in verse, the latter especially in certain poetic forms based on syllable counts, accents, and rhyme schemes which have a particular relation to and influence on the musical patterns associated with them.

The musical form associated with dialogue is the recitative; that associated with monologue is the aria—under which term for the moment may be comprised also the duet, trio, quartet, and ensemble—but not the chorus. In fact, there are hardly any choruses in Scarlatti's operas; the few examples are limited for the most part to brief outbursts, eight or twelve measures in length, purely homophonic in style and musically insignificant. One is tempted to think of them as designed to be sung by the stagehands or other extras in the crowd scenes, who could easily have been taught them by rote. As for the words, practically all that a chorus ever does is to confirm or applaud decisions already taken by their betters. We may perhaps see in the status of the chorus in these operas a reflection of the role regarded as proper for the common people in the order of contemporary society.

A great deal of ignorant depreciation has been expended on the recitative of eighteenth-century opera—perhaps inspired by often quoted statements of contemporary observers who report that the audiences never bothered to listen to the recitatives but used them as cover for conversation, card playing, and so on, reserving their attention solely for the arias. This may indeed have been the case, particularly since the words of the recitatives in the theatre do go past extremely rapidly and, furthermore, since anyone who wanted to could easily read them from the printed librettos which were always furnished. But the recitatives in Scarlatti are not by any means without musical interest, as I hope we shall hear from some examples later on.

There are two distinct kinds of recitative in these operas. The more common is called in modern terminology *recitativo secco* (literally "dry recitative") or, more correctly in eighteenth-century terminology, *recitativo semplice* ("simple recitative"): it is so called because it has no regular rhythmic pulse and no balanced melodic form and also because it is not accompanied by the orchestra but only by the harpsichord and a sustaining bass instrument, usually a violoncello. It is evident that one has to define this recitative mainly in negative terms. It may be understood as being the thinnest possible musical covering of a text, a covering so thin, in fact, that the shape of the language shows through everywhere. Jean Baptiste Lully, the first great composer of French opera, claimed that he used to model his recitatives on the declamation of the actors at the Comédie-Française in order to obtain a dramatically valid musical rendition of his texts. I have not heard that Scarlatti ever resorted to a similar procedure, but his simple recitatives do very strongly suggest models, conscious or unconscious, in the declamation of the Italian theatre—not so much, probably, the literary theatre of serious Italian drama as the popular theatre in the tradition of the commedia dell'arte.

Contrasting with the *recitativo semplice* are occasional short passages of *recitativo accompagnato* or (in the more common contemporary terminology) *recitativo obbligato*, that is, recitative accompanied by instruments, meaning the full string orchestra including always the double basses. This kind of recitative is reserved for places of exceptional solemnity or for highly charged emotional passages, or (characteristically) for the so-called *ombra* scenes, apparitions of the dead delivering messages of sombre import.

Without too much inaccuracy it may be said that in recitative the action moves and the music stands still, whereas in the aria the reverse obtains: the action stops and the music takes over. Recitative is specific, aria is general. Every aria is a musical response to the stimulus of a particular situation. This extremely sharp distinction of recitative and aria, it must be said, is more characteristic of Scarlatti's later works than of his early ones. In the operas before 1700, and especially in the Roman operas of the early 1680s, one often finds an intermingling, or rather an interpenetration, of recitative and aria styles. We shall come to examples of these later on: meanwhile (on the principle that the true nature of anything is best understood from its state at the point of its highest development) let us consider the aria as we find it from *Eraclea,* which dates from 1700, nearly at the end of Scarlatti's first Neapolitan period, to *Griselda,* his last surviving opera, produced at Rome in January of 1721.

The most striking feature of the poetry for these arias is a clear division into two parts, of approximately equal length. Typically, the last line of the second part (which we may call part B) rhymes with the last line of part A. In part A the singer is saying, in effect, "this is how I feel about the present situation" or else "the present situation gives rise to the following thoughts in my mind." In part B he may expand on the idea expressed in part A, or turn it around a little so as to view it from a different angle, or perhaps suggest a related but slightly contrasting idea. For example, here are the words of the aria "Spesso il ciel" from *La principessa fedele,* performed at Naples in 1710:

A.	Spesso il Ciel sembra sdegnato	a	8
	E placato	a	4
	Poi non scaglia le saette;	b	8
B.	Ma talor, che sembra in pace,	c	8
	Più vivace,	c	4
	Mostra poi le sue vendette.	b	8

> Often Heaven seems hostile
>   And then, appeased,
>   Does not shoot its arrows;
> But sometimes, when it seems peaceful,
>   It then more vigorously
>   Shoots forth its vengefulness.

In the musical setting of such a text part A typically is longer than part B—perhaps twice as long. Such expansion is achieved by the ritornellos (orchestral introductions and interludes) and partly by expansion of the vocal part itself, involving repetitions of the text and ever-lengthening phrases, usually with passages of coloratura. Thus for this particular aria (see example 1) we find the following formal scheme:

PART A:	Orchestra	4+4 mm.	
	Voice	5+6 mm., 1 m. interlude	44
		4+6 mm., then 8 mm. to a cadence	measures
	Orchestra	6 mm.	
PART B:	Voice	4+8 mm.	22
		4+6 mm.	measures

PART A: repeated, without the opening ritornello

This same example illustrates another typical feature of the aria form in Scarlatti, namely the key scheme. Thus the opening ritornello establishes the main tonality of G major; the first period of the voice part cadences in the dominant D major, whence the second returns to the tonic G and confirms it for eight more measures; then the closing ritornello, starting with a brief reference to the dominant harmony reconfirms the tonic key of G. (This ritornello is a telescoped repetition of the first one.) The second part of the aria modulates to the relative E minor in the first half and then cadences in the mediant B minor at the end of the second half, after which we go back to G major for the repetition of part I. This relationship mediant minor–tonic major is usual for all Scarlatti's arias in major keys.

It is also typical of these operas that this aria is short: the performing time is about three and a half minutes. To us the word *aria* is more likely to suggest something like "Il mio tesoro" or "Un bel dì"—at any rate, something nearly twice as long as this. But the majority of arias in Scarlatti, as in the operas of other Italian composers of his time, are of what seem to us rather small dimensions. As the eighteenth century went on, opera arias tended to become fewer and longer. J. A. Hasse's *Ruggiero,* performed in 1771, has seventeen arias; Scarlatti's *Eraclea* (1700) has fifty-seven, and his *Griselda* (1721) has forty-one. Bearing in mind that there are recitatives between the arias and (usually) also ballets between the acts, and that the total performance time for a whole Scarlatti opera was probably not much more than three hours, we come out (on a very rough calculation) with an average length of less than three minutes per aria for *Eraclea* and about three and a half for *Griselda*. Such dimensions are probably typical for all Italian operas of the time.

Now, to continue this arithmetic through one more step, consider that neither Scarlatti nor his Italian contemporaries ever had to compose an entire aria but only three-fifths of one. They composed part A and part B, and then placed under the last measure of part B the words "da capo"—go back to the beginning and sing part A over again. (This little fact may help to explain how eighteenth-century composers could write so many operas as they did.)

This brings up the subject not only of the da capo aria in eighteenth-century Italian opera but of the function in general of repetition as an element in musical design. Repetition, literal or modified, is basic in nearly all types of Western music—least obvious in older forms going back to medieval practice such as plainchant and the sixteenth-century motet, most obvious in dance music and the early shorter vocal forms based on poetic structures such as the fourteenth-century madrigal, the ballade, or the virelai. In general, repetition may be literal (as of the two sections of a minuet in a classical symphony) or modified (as in a theme and variations); it may be immediate (as in these two cases), or it may come after something contrasting has been heard (as with the repetition of the minuet after the trio in a classical symphony); or repetition, either literal or modified, may be a continuous or nearly continuous element in the musical texture (as with the subject in a fugue or the series of intervals in a work based on a tone row). And of course all these different kinds of repetition may be combined and modified in an indefinite number of ways. The musical "meaning" of a composition, or section of a composition, insofar as that meaning depends upon the device of repetition, obviously will be different depending on what kinds of repetition are involved. A da capo aria clearly involves repetition after contrast (part A is heard again after part B), and as far as the written score is concerned the repetition seems to be literal—at any rate, certainly, a literal repetition of the words. The singer is saying in part A "this is how I feel about the present situation"; when he comes to part B he introduces it with an implied connective, either "furthermore" or "however"; when he goes back to part A he implies either "nevertheless" or "and, as I said before." He has made a statement, he has expanded or commented on it, and he has repeated it. The repetition has added nothing to the original statement, nor does it suggest the possibility of any other statement to follow. Everything is neatly tied up and, for the moment at least, there is nothing more to be said.

Of course, as everyone knows, the da capo repetition in eighteenth-century opera arias was not perfectly exact as regards the music. Every singer was expected to add ornaments to the written melodic line—trills, appoggiaturas, passing tones, cadenzas—some at the first time through and more at the da capo repetition. As expressed by one contemporary writer the requirements were as follows:

"Among the things worthy of Consideration, the first to be taken Notice of, is the Manner in which all *Airs* divided into three Parts are to be sung. In the first they require nothing but the simplest Ornaments, of a good Taste and few, that the Composition may remain simple, plain, and pure; in the second they expect, that to this Purity some artful Graces be added, by which the Judicious may hear, that the Ability of the Singer is greater; and, in repeating the *Air*, he that does not vary it for the better, is no great Master."[4]

4. P. F. Tosi, *Opinioni de' cantori antichi, e moderni, o sieno Osservazioni sopra il canto figurato* (Bologna: L. dalla Volpe, 1723); trans. J. E. Galliard as *Observations on the Florid Song; or, Sentiments on the Ancient and Modern Singers* (London: J. Wilcox, 1742, 2d. ed. 1743; reprint ed., London, 1926), pp. 93–94.

A notorious critic and satirist, Benedetto Marcello, has been the source of a great deal of exaggeration about abuses in the performance of eighteenth-century Italian opera. Without going into citations from his famous *Teatro alla moda,* the general trend of which is sufficiently well known, I suggest two or three considerations in connection with this work. In the first place, as its comic dedication clearly suggests, it is a humorous essay, a parody or satire, indeed a burlesque; and this kind of writing always involves the unabashed use of exaggeration and the citing of particular instances (real or imaginary) in such a way as to suggest that they are typical, whereas in fact they are more likely to be exceptional. In the second place, Marcello himself was a disappointed opera composer; his four or five attempts in that genre seem to have had no success whatever. He published his *Teatro alla moda* under an obviously comic pseudonym. (As the King of Hearts said, "You must have meant some mischief, or else you'd have signed your name like an honest man.") The whole essay owed its contemporary popular success to its comic verve and exaggeration; and it is not the least of tributes to its success as a joke that it has been solemnly quoted by nearly all writers for the last 250 years as if it were a sober factual account of things as they really were in the opera houses of eighteenth-century Italy. No doubt practices of the sort Marcello caricatures did exist, but certainly any such abuses must have been more prevalent in the popular opera houses of Marcello's own city of Venice than in the aristocratically controlled theatres of Rome and Naples where Scarlatti chiefly worked.

It is true that Scarlatti, like all his contemporaries (and like all later eighteenth-century composers, including Mozart), took very careful account of the singers who were going to perform his works. This we can gather from passages in his correspondence with the prince Ferdinando de' Medici in the years 1702 to 1706, as also from the many changes he made in his original score of *Griselda* when the promising young castrato Carestini was engaged at the last minute to take a part in this opera at Rome. But the abuses perpetrated by eighteenth-century singers, the capricious distortions of which Metastasio so bitterly complained and of which so much has been written since, apparently were not nearly so serious in Scarlatti's time as they may later have become.

With this reservation, we return to the simple fact that the da capo aria in Scarlatti's operas is an example of a musical form based on repetition after contrast; it is repetition modified only by the addition of external melodic embellishments which were not written in the score but introduced at will by the individual performer and which moreover need not have been identical at every performance. The ornaments as such were obligatory by custom; their exact shape was a matter for personal choice, but they were rigidly confined within the limits set by the composer's score. In short, embellishments at the repetition add nothing essential to the initial musical idea. As with the words, so with the music; a statement is made, a supplementary statement follows, and then the first statement is repeated, confirmed. Simply because the repetition in itself added nothing substantially new, a need may have been felt to disguise this fact by means of superficial ornament.

The ornaments, however, do serve the purpose of injecting into the performance of an aria a certain element of the unforeseeable. As everyone knows who has investigated many arias in the operas of Scarlatti and his contemporaries, once the first ten or twelve measures have been heard it is not difficult to foresee (in a very general way, of course) what is going to happen: the formal outlines, the proportions, and the course of the modulations are basically alike in all these arias. What cannot be anticipated, however, are the details, and among these details is the way in which the singer is going to ornament the melody and add his cadenzas, particularly if he chooses, as he normally would, to do these differently at every performance. It is perhaps this fact which, as much as any other, accounts for the overwhelming importance allotted to the singers in contemporary accounts of eighteenth-century operas.

Considered as a whole, then, it is evident that in the operas of Scarlatti and his contemporaries libretto and music perfectly correspond: in both, dramatic movement alternates with static contemplation. The da capo aria is thus the only appropriate, indeed the only possible, musical form for the kind of drama exemplified in the librettos from which Scarlatti worked.

It may be worthwhile to consider for a moment what happens to the idea of repetition as an element of musical form in the course of the late eighteenth century: to contrast, for example, the return of the first part of a da capo aria in a Scarlatti opera with the recapitulation in a Haydn or Beethoven symphony. The trend of the time was away from vocal music and toward instrumental music, and by the end of the century there had been added to this the effort to make instrumental music itself dramatic, to express without words the movement of dramatic tension and resolution which formerly—insofar as it had been desired at all—had required for expression both music and words. Thus the recapitulation in Beethoven is more than just repetition after contrast; it is also the dramatic climax of the movement, carefully prepared and led up to through the development section. The musical theme, though still recognizably that with which the movement began, no longer "says" quite the same thing that it said before. Its recurrence is not merely repetition, but also a new and climactic stage in the unfolding of an inner drama. Is it merely fanciful to suggest regarding the dawn of an age in which for the first time it began to be accepted that the social status of a child need not always and forever be the same as that of his parents, that this same age was the one in which it first dawned upon composers that the repetition of a musical theme need not always and necessarily be only a decorated replica of its original statement?

To exemplify a complete da capo aria we take another from Scarlatti's opera *La principessa fedele* (see example 2). This aria is of a kind that he used fairly frequently in his operas for the expression of sorrowful, pathetic feelings: it is in a minor key (E minor, Scarlatti's favorite key for arias of this type), in a slow tempo (specifically marked *lento*), with triple subdivision of the beat making a rhythm similar to that of a barcarolle; and it is marked by a recurring chromatic inflection of the melodic line, the lowered second degree (producing a chord known as the "Neapolitan sixth"), which is heard especially at the approach to cadences. This aria occurs toward the end of the first act. The dramatic situation of the opera at this point is a little complicated. Cunegonde, its heroine, is a predecessor of Fidelio in Beethoven's opera. She has come, disguised as a young man, to rescue her betrothed husband

Ridolfo who has been captured and is being held as a slave at the court of the sultan of Egypt. Not daring of course to reveal either her own or Ridolfo's identity, she nevertheless manages, in the course of a long and animated scene in recitative, to obtain permission to talk with him. The words of her aria are addressed ostensibly to the other characters in the scene, but actually, of course, to the audience; and at the end of the aria, in accordance with the usual custom, she makes her exit.

Quando poi vedrai lo strale	a	8
Ch'ho nel sen n'avrai pietà.	b	7
Che scoprir piaga mortale,	a	8
Nè sanarla, è crudeltà.	b	7

When you shall see the arrow
    Which I have in my bosom,
    you will have pity on it.
For to uncover a mortal wound
    And not to heal it, is cruelty.

·*II*·

Rome and the Early Operas
1679–1684

Pietro Alessandro Gaspare Scarlatti was born at Palermo on 2 May 1660, second of the eight children of Pietro Scarlata and his wife, Eleonora d'Amato. Nothing certain is known about the parents or about the boy's early musical education. No conservatory training in music was available in Palermo at this time; the child Alessandro may have been taught the rudiments by a presumed relative of his mother, Don Vincenzo Amato, a musician of some note who was *maestro di cappella* at the local cathedral. Undoubtedly the young Scarlatti showed enough signs of exceptional talent that his parents decided to send him to Rome where he could be adequately trained and where he might, with luck, make "contacts" which would be helpful if not indispensable for his future career. Such a procedure was not uncommon at the time for families with talented children (nor is it, of course, unknown today). One might have expected that nearby Naples would have been the parents' choice; but Naples was not yet the celebrated musical center that it was later to become—largely thanks to Scarlatti himself. Moreover, there were other reasons for the choice of Rome. Vincenzo Amato had connections there, and it seems possible also that Alessandro's family had relatives there. No positive evidence has yet been found for this, but there certainly were at the time families in Rome named Scarlatti, and it may have been into the care of one of these households that the twelve-year-old Alessandro, together with two of his younger sisters, was shipped off in June of 1672.

By what route those three children travelled, whether any older person went with them, and just what they were expected to do when they arrived—these are matters for romantic fiction. Not one scrap of reliable information has yet been turned up either about the voyage or about the events of the next five years. Did the young boy from Sicily have lessons with the most famous musician then living in Rome, Giacomo Carissimi? Legend says so, but there is no proof; in any case, the course could not have been a long one, for Carissimi died in January of 1674 at the age of sixty-eight. Did Scarlatti study at one of the numerous choir schools connected with the great Roman churches and seminaries? Again: possible but unproved. The only certainty is that he made rapid progress both in the art of music and in the cultivation of influential friends. By 1677 he is composing a little opera— perhaps an earlier version of *La Rosmene*—for a soirée at the house of one of his patrons. In January of 1679 he is commissioned to compose an oratorio; the document calls him "il Scarlattino alias il Siciliano." Meanwhile in 1678, two weeks before his eighteenth birthday, he is married to a young Roman woman, Antonia Anzalone; of the ten children eventually born of this marriage only five lived to maturity—a typical survival rate for the time. In the marriage record his name is spelled for the first time as we know it, with two *t*'s. The family name in Sicily was Scarlata or Sgarlata; at Rome, and even later, it sometimes appears as Scarlati. Perhaps the final, definitive spelling was adopted to conform to that of Roman relatives—or perhaps, as has been suggested, to claim a relationship which did not in fact exist.

In order to understand Scarlatti's career and his operas it is helpful to know something about the institution of patronage in seventeenth-century Italy. Opera, of course, like all expensive kinds of music—but more so than any other—has always been dependent on patrons. Of the two classes of musical patrons in Italy, one, the church, seldom encouraged opera and indeed sometimes actively opposed it. Opera depended therefore on a few wealthy members of the noble class who for one reason or another were willing to take it upon themselves to foot the bills. This was the case even in the "free republic" of Venice, and much more decidedly so in the autocratically governed states of Rome, Naples, and Florence.

Rome at this time was in some respects a particularly favorable place for a talented and ambitious young composer. Already for forty years before Scarlatti's time, opera both serious and comic had flourished there, chiefly under the patronage of the Barberini family, princes of the church. And it was now another prince of the church, Cardinal Benedetto Pamphili, who became Scarlatti's first powerful and generous protector. The life story of this extraordinary potentate reads like a fairy tale; one might almost believe that Edgar Allen Poe had Pamphili's career in mind as an instance of the ideally happy life which he describes in his sketch "The Domain of Arnheim":

> From his cradle to his grave a gale of prosperity bore my friend Ellison along. Nor do I use the word prosperity in its mere worldly sense. I mean it as synonymous with happiness. The person of whom I speak seemed born for the purpose of . . . exemplifying by individual instance what has been deemed the chimera of the perfectionists. . . . In his existence I fancy that I have seen refuted the dogma that in man's very nature lies some hidden principle, the antagonist of bliss. An anxious examination of his career has given me to understand . . . that as a species we have in our possession the as yet unwrought elements of content—and that, even now in the present darkness and madness of all thought on the great question of the social condition, it is not impossible that man, the individual, under certain unusual and highly fortuitous conditions may be happy.

The "unusual and highly fortuitous conditions" that Poe postulated for his imaginary friend were, of course, quite different from the actual conditions of Cardinal Pamphili's life.[1] Born in 1653 into one of the oldest, wealthiest, and most highly connected of Roman families, educated in all the noble sports and accomplishments of youth, baccalaureate in philosophy at twenty-three and cardinal at twenty-eight, poet and author of texts of numerous cantatas and oratorios, trusted ambassador and dip-

---

1. Lina Montalto, *Un mecenate in Roma barocca: il cardinale Benedetto Pamphilij (1653–1730)* (Florence: Sansoni, 1955).

lomatic agent of reigning popes, head of the Vatican Library which he enriched with important manuscript acquisitions, munificent patron of arts and letters on a scale outstanding even for that time and place, it would seem that Pamphili lacked nothing that could make for human happiness. In his own palace—or rather, in the principal one of his half-dozen residences in Rome and vicinity—he maintained a staff of over one hundred household servants and officials, a resident orchestra as well as numerous outside musicians and poets, and a library with a collection of hundreds of precious books and manuscripts, including manuscripts of music copied professionally on his own premises. He bought horses and carriages the way a modern billionaire buys Chryslers and Cadillacs—twenty-five new horses in the one season of 1671–72, for example. The price of a fine horse at this time was around 300 scudi, while the monthly stipend of a musician was seven scudi (plus board and room, of course), so that such a person might, if he saved his entire salary, accumulate enough in about four years to buy himself a horse—that is, if he had any place to keep it or any servants to take care of it or any money left over to buy grain and hay for it.

So much for the crudely economic aspect of patronage, but this of course is only one side of the story. A large part of the works of public charity, aid to the poor, hospitals, education, and many other needs for which we now rely either on the state or the semiprivate, semipublic foundations and similar agencies—a great many of these things were the responsibility of wealthy individuals; and to judge from the surviving records of his household accounts, Cardinal Benedetto Pamphili more than measured up to that responsibility. He was munificent not only in his own household and to the many poets, savants, artists, and musicians whom he supported, but to literally hundreds of humbler persons as well.

In any case, as far as Scarlatti is concerned, we do not need to suppose that the young musician was financially dependent altogether on patrons. He had other sources of income as well—probably, for example, from his employment as *maestro di cappella* or assistant *maestro* in one or two of the Roman churches. From a document of 1681 it appears that at the time Scarlatti was living in the Strada Felice with a household consisting of his wife, two infant children, his sister-in-law, a nurse, and his brother Giuseppe. Nevertheless, whatever his financial circumstances, it still was chiefly to his patrons that Scarlatti had to look for advancement in his chosen career. The money he received from them, whether regularly as salary or periodically as special gifts in return for the composition of cantatas, serenatas, oratorios, or operas, was less important than the advantage of living constantly in an atmosphere of encouragement, in company with such notable colleagues as Pasquini and Corelli, working in collaboration with the best available professional musicians and singers, always with the supreme incentive of knowing that what he produced would be performed—and performed under his own supervision, for audiences capable of understanding and appreciating it. Such were the audiences assembled as guests in Cardinal Pamphili's palace at concerts held weekly or oftener during the Carnival seasons. Scarlatti's first three operas were heard by audiences of this kind, under private auspices, before being presented at the public theatres.

Cardinal Pamphili was not Scarlatti's only patron at Rome. Another cardinal, Pietro Ottoboni, grandnephew of Pope Alexander VIII, took an interest in him from the beginning. These two noblemen entered into virtual rivalry for the presentation of operas—all in open defiance of the reigning Pope Innocent XI who, convinced that the theatre was a hotbed of immorality, was doing everything possible to discourage plays and operas. So the two cardinals erected quite sizeable and very well-equipped private theatres in their palaces, invited their friends, and proceeded to stage one opera after another. Cardinal Ottoboni moreover continued to befriend Scarlatti even after the latter's departure from Rome in 1684. It was this patron who wrote the libretto and commissioned the music for Scarlatti's *Statira* in 1690; later he became Scarlatti's main reliance in the years of hardship at Rome after 1702. It was Ottoboni also who engaged Filippo Juvarra as his theatre architect and commissioned for Rome in 1712 Scarlatti's opera *Ciro,* for which Juvarra designed the stage sets.

The most picturesque of all Scarlatti's patrons at Rome in the 1680s was that signally liberated woman, Queen Christina of Sweden. This illustrious and politically important convert to Catholicism had renounced her throne and travelled to Italy in 1655 in what amounted to a triumphal journey across Europe. After stopping off at Innsbruck for a special performance in her honor of Cesti's *Argia,* Christina made her entry into Rome just before Christmas, escorted by an endless string of carriages and welcomed to a brilliant reception at the Pamphili palace and an almost immediate interview with the newly elected Pope Alexander VII Chigi. Even before she finally settled permanently at Rome in 1668, Christina had made her presence strongly felt. Not only the ruling authorities but also artistic and literary circles were soon dominated by her strong personality; the whole world of art and literature at Rome seems to have revolved about her. She was a student of the Latin classics and of Italian literature who had written learned essays on Cyrus, Alexander, and Caesar. She was interested in science, in astrology and magic. She had a laboratory in her palace where she experimented with the transmutation of metals. Her sharp critical intellect enabled her to select infallibly the brilliant circle of poets, musicians, artists, and savants who gathered in her salon and who became the nucleus of the Arcadia, that most famous of Rome's many academies. Lina Montalto sees in Christina an instance of that mysterious pull of the Latin genius on the mystic and fantastic genius of the north, her coming to Rome not merely a religious conversion but an instance of the moth attracted by the flame. But unlike the moth in the flame, Christina was fully at home in Roman society. She was present— naturally—at the first performance of Scarlatti's *Equivoci nel sembiante* in 1679; in the libretto of his *Honestà negli amori* of 1680 we are informed that the twenty-year-old composer was already Queen Christina's *maestro di cappella,* a post he retained even after his departure for Naples three years later. Pasquini's operas *Alcasta* (1673) and *Lisimaco* (1681) are dedicated to Christina; so are Corelli's Trio Sonatas op. 1 of 1683 and Scarlatti's opera *Pompeo* of the same year.

Among other active patrons of music and opera at Rome was Lorenzo Onofrio Colonna, the "Gran Contestabile" whose palace was the scene of many concerts, cantatas, and new operas in the 1670s and '80s. Scarlatti's *Pompeo* had its premiere there in 1683.

In the records concerning these private theatres we often find mention simply of "*commedie*," literally comedies but more generally signifying simply plays or dramas—probably in some cases actual operas, since the word *commedia* was used also as meaning *commedia in musica*, a play in (or with) music.

There were also two public theatres in Rome, though these led a rather precarious existence owing to the frequent opposition of the popes. The Teatro di Tordinona, constructed in 1660, reopened and refurbished in 1671, was finally completely dismantled and permanently closed by Pope Innocent XII in 1692 as part of his determined campaign to put an end to public theatrical spectacles. Six years later the pope likewise closed the other Roman public theatre, the Teatro Capranica. In particular, the popes objected to the use of their own choir singers for secular dramatic performances, and most emphatically so when their castrati had to appear on the stage in female costume. On the whole, one can only say that if there was much foundation in fact for the conditions of backstage morals as painted in the famous fourth satire of Lodovico Adimari (published in 1716 but said to have been written in the 1690s),[2] or if some of the stories about the women opera singers of Naples in the same period were true (which there is no special reason to doubt), the attitude of the antitheatrical popes is understandable.

Although we know nothing about Scarlatti's early formal training in music, we do know a fair amount about something that is equally if not more important for his development as a composer, namely the music that he must have heard in Rome between the twelfth and twenty-fourth years of his age. This included, first, church music—motets, masses either in the *stile antico* (the strict or "Palestrina" style) or in the newer *stile concertato* for soloists and chorus with orchestra; second, cantatas, which were fluttering continually through the elegant salons of Rome like birds in springtime; third, instrumental music such as the keyboard works of Pasquini or the trio sonatas of Corelli; fourth, oratorios, sacred

2. Lodovico Adimari, "Satira quarta: contro alcuni vizi delle donne, e particolarmente contro le cantatrice," in *Satire del marchese Lodovico Adimari* (Livorno: T. Masi, 1788), pp. 183–253.

in subject matter (though not liturgical), performed in chapels, churches, or private music rooms, many of them quasi-operatic in form, and substituting as it were for opera in certain seasons of the year, especially in Lent; and finally operas or near-operas, ranging from unpretentious little *commedie in musica* to full-scale operatic productions for the large theatres, private or public. It is worth remembering that Scarlatti continued to compose in all these genres throughout his life, such was the impetus of those early impressionable years at Rome. He was no more a mere specialist in opera than was Mozart.

Turning now however to our more specific concern, let us inquire as to what operas the young Scarlatti could have seen and heard at Rome in the years from 1672 to 1684. As was usual in Italy at this time, the repertoire consisted for the most part of works by local composers—works moreover which played only for one or two seasons and were seldom revived afterward. Cesti had lived in Rome sporadically in the early 1660s; his opera *La Dori* was revived there in 1672 and perhaps again in 1680, always with the customary changes and additions. Scarlatti may have heard *La Dori* and possibly three or four operas of Sartorio and other Venetians which found their way to Rome around this time, but it is unlikely that the Venetian style had much if any direct influence on his earliest works for the stage. However, there is considerable evidence for a "late Roman" school of opera in the last three decades of the seventeenth century, represented chiefly by Bernardo Pasquini (1637–1710; better known for his keyboard works) and that erratic genius Alessandro Stradella (1644–1682); and it seems likely that these were the composers whose works chiefly served as models for Scarlatti's earliest operas.[3]

Probably his first opera was *Gli equivoci nel sembiante,* which had its premiere in the private theatre of still another of Scarlatti's Roman patrons, the architect and Abbé Domenico Filippo Contini (who was, incidentally, the author of the libretto) sometime in January or early February of 1679. Present on this occasion, of course, was Queen Christina, to whose influence it was probably due that the opera was almost immediately taken up at the theatre

3. See Carolyn Gianturco, "Evidence for a Late Roman School of Opera," *Music & Letters,* 56 (1975): 4–13.

in the Collegio Clementino and soon afterward at the Teatro Capranica. On the former occasion there was a small riot at the entrance of the theatre. Evidently the pope had given orders that Scarlatti himself was not to be admitted to the Collegio Clementino—for reasons which we may speculate about presently—and this prohibition must have threatened the success of the opera, since according to custom it was the composer who had to preside at the harpsichord and direct the performance. With her usual promptness and decision, Queen Christina intervened. She sent her carriage to bring Scarlatti to the theatre, but this was not all. Cardinal Colonna had placed some of his armed retainers at the queen's service. At her orders, these bravos forced their way through the Papal Guards at the door (not without beating up a number of guards in the process) and saw to it that Scarlatti took his place at the harpsichord. The queen listened to the opera tranquilly from Cardinal Colonna's box.

Gli equivochi had a wide success that was altogether exceptional for an opera at this time. Within two years it had made its way to Bologna, Naples, Monte Filottrano, and Vienna; subsequently it was heard at Ravenna and Palermo, always with the usual changes and substitutions and often with changes of title. Scarlatti himself seems to have been present for the Vienna performances in the Carnival season of 1681, and this excursion may also have involved a visit to Munich (for which, however, no certain evidence has yet turned up); at any rate, this is the only known occasion on which the composer ever set foot outside Italy.

The extraordinary success of this first opera of Scarlatti's—success on a scale hardly to be equalled by any of his later works—is attributable to a number of factors. First of all, the music itself is melodious and attractive, in a style very well suited to the simple pastoral plot. Secondly, the work could be easily staged: it makes no exceptional demands in the way of virtuosity on the part of the four singers, and requires only a small orchestra and no expensive stage sets or elaborate machinery for spectacular effects. But it is impossible to avoid the impression that still another and even more powerful influence was at work here, namely fashion. As we all know, the reputation of a young composer (or any young artist) often shoots up in the most ex-

Cast of *Gli equivoci nel sembiante,*
University of California, Los Angeles, production, 1975
COURTESY OF THE DEPARTMENT OF MUSIC.

traordinary way—and, unfortunately, often falls back as fast as it went up. Something of this kind seems to have happened in the case of Scarlatti. The enthusiasm of his illustrious Roman patrons—and especially, no doubt, that of Queen Christina—seems to have spread almost instantly to other aristocratic circles which were, so to speak, in communion with the aristocracy of Rome, and the unknown twenty-year-old genius from the remote world of Sicily suddenly found himself fashionable.

The title *Gli equivoci nel sembiante* is awkwardly translatable as "Misunderstandings due to appearances"—the word *sembiante* meaning both "appearance" in the ordinary sense and "countenance" or the "looks" or "appearance" of a person's face. Doubtless the play on this word is intentional, as the plot would indicate. The work is a little pastorale in three acts, for two sopranos and two tenors and an orchestra of first and second violins (occasionally plus viola, as in No. 19) with basso continuo. The action (such as it is) revolves about a double misunderstanding and case of mistaken identity. Clori, a shepherdess, is in love with Eurillo, a shepherd. Clori's sister Lisetta starts all the trouble by inserting a couple of words in a letter which Clori has written; she is able to do this while Clori is sleeping (Clori is the first of a long line of Scarlatti's heroines who never seem able to stay awake throughout an entire opera). Misunderstandings, quarrels, and mutual reproaches multiply. Clori mistakes a certain stranger Armindo for Eurillo, and this of course leads to more trouble. Finally Lisetta confesses her trick and Armindo turns out to be Eurillo's twin brother. Clori gets Eurillo, Lisetta gets Armindo, and all ends happily.

Quite different from *Gli equivoci nel sembiante* was Scarlatti's second opera *L'honestà negli amori,* first performed at a private theatre at Rome in 1680 and evidently taken up at only two other cities much later: Siena in 1690 and Genoa in 1705—a marked contrast to the immediate and widespread acclaim enjoyed by its predecessor. *L'honestà* can perhaps best be described as a romantic melodrama, replete with pirates, desert islands, desperate love affairs, mistaken identities, and comic interludes, with the usual display of magnanimity and a happy ending. The variety of musical form in the arias of this work is remarkable; it is perhaps the least stereotyped in this respect of all Scarlatti's operas. Both Dent and Lorenz praise this variety and speak highly of the expressive power of many of the individual numbers; but it may well be that it was precisely this originality, this (so to call it) extravagant treatment of the libretto, disappointing to the expectations of the hearers, that worked against the contemporary success of *L'honestà*. Notably, however, this work was revived in 1966 for a performance celebrating the 300th anniversary of the then lately restored Drottningholm Court Theatre at Stockholm.

Better success greeted the *commedia musicale* entitled *Tutto il mal non vien per nuocere* ("Not every misfortune is harmful") of 1681, which after playing at Rome in the public Teatro Capranica and then privately, made its way within the next five years to Ancona, Siena, Ravenna, Florence, and finally in 1687 to the viceroy's palace at Naples, this time under the title *Dal male il bene*. It is a curious circumstance that the only two surviving complete scores of this opera are not found in any of the cities where it was performed; one is in the Monastery of Montecassino and other in the Deutsche Staatsbibliothek in Berlin. The Montecassino score is evidently autograph with the addition (also in Scarlatti's hand) of a comic prologue, a sinfonia (overture), and three new arias for the Naples performances. The Berlin score is a contemporary copy with violas added to the orchestral parts; it was probably prepared for the performances at Florence in 1686. The new title at Naples was perhaps an allusion to Marazzoli's and Abbatini's opera *Dal male il bene* (Rome, 1653), the libretto of which was by the same Giulio Rospigliosi who later became a cardinal and eventually pope under the title Clement IX. The plot of Scarlatti's opera is nothing but a series of misunderstandings, disguises, defiances, deception, and desperation, enlivened periodically by quarrels and lovemaking between the two comic servants, and with everything of course coming out all right in the final scene. Scarlatti's music, or at any rate a good deal of it, is much better than the silly libretto deserves.

Il Pompeo is Scarlatti's earliest *dramma per musica* or at any rate the earliest of which a score survives. It was first performed at Colonna's private theatre in January of 1683, made its way to Naples just one year later, and subsequently was heard at four other Italian cities, including Palermo (the composer's birthplace) in 1690. *Pompeo* is on the same libretto (by Nicolò Minato) to which Cavalli had composed music for Venice in 1666. Scarlatti's music, on the whole, is conservative in style and much of it not very distinguished. He could and did cope with the little pastoral scenes of *Gli equivoci nel sembiante* and the playful comedy of *Tutto il mal non vien per nuocere,* but the horrors of the grim and tortuous world of ancient Roman politics confronted him with a new challenge. Nevertheless, *Pompeo* is of interest as showing how its twenty-two-year-old composer, working generally within the frame of established tradition of this kind of musical drama, managed to infuse that tradition with a certain amount of life; and at the same time we find a foretaste of the later Scarlatti both in some technical details of the music and in some of the larger aspects of the musical form.

The plot of *Pompeo* is of a kind which had become common in Italian serious operas of the seventeenth-century Venetian school and which was to remain standard for such works throughout nearly the whole of the eighteenth century. Mozart's *Clemenza di Tito* is the best known late example of this kind of plot, which may be briefly described as a free fantasia on historical themes. The historical Pompey had defeated the armies of Mitridates VI in 65 B.C. and reduced his kingdom of Pontus to a Roman province. Mitridates committed suicide two years later. When Pompey entered Rome in 61 he was greeted with a magnificent "triumph." He was associated with Caesar and Crassus in the First Triumvirate and married Caesar's daughter Giulia. So much for the historical facts; now let us see what Scarlatti's librettist made out of them.

The opera opens with the scene of Pompeo's triumphal entry into Rome; a chorus of soldiers hails him in six measures of homophonic "vivas" and then subsides into the background. (The chorus emerges in a few later scenes of the opera but seldom has anything particular to say, its function being only decorative.) Pompeo displays the captives he has brought back with him. He and his son Sesto are astonished to find among the captives Isicratea and Farnace, respectively wife and son of the conquered Mitridate. Pompeo, in a burst of magnanimity, apologizes to them and releases them. In the next two scenes the lovemaking begins: first Sesto then Claudio approach Isicratea with loving words, but she repulses them both. We then see Mitridate who, it seems, has escaped from his captors and come to Rome in disguise, determined to assassinate Pompeo if possible. He laments his situation in two arias, separated by a recitative. After two more love scenes (Giulia-Scipione, Giulia-Pompeo) we return to Mitridate; just as he is about to reveal himself secretly to his wife, Isicratea's two lovers barge in: Sesto becomes hopeful, but Claudio laments in despair. Then, after another love argument between Pompeo and the still reluctant Giulia (who, of course, loves Scipione) and a quasi-comic episode between Sesto and the slave Harpalia, comes the recognition scene between Mitridate and Isicratea. Mitridate then conceals himself while Pompeo enters with Farnace. When Pompeo promises to befriend the young Farnace, Mitridate resolves not to assassinate him after all; but Pompeo, still troubled by his unrequited love for Giulia, goes to sleep to think it over, whereupon Mitridate emerges in order to carry out his fell design, but is dissuaded by Farnace who apparently does not yet recognize his father. This scene ends the first act.

Act II begins with another attempt by Pompeo to soften Giulia's heart. Scipione magnanimously offers to give her up to Pompeo, but she objects. Pompeo is next shown, with a chorus of soldiers, about to march off to further victories. Caesar, in his only aria of the opera, urges them on; but Pompeo confides to the audience in an aria that he cares nothing for glory if he cannot have Giulia's love. Meanwhile, Sesto tries to enlist the slave Harpalia to further his dastardly designs on Isicratea, who still steadfastly spurns his love and once more dismisses him with contumely. Mitridate ("*in disparte*") overhears her final words to Sesto and, with the usual credulity of operatic husbands, concludes that his wife is contemplating infidelity; she repels his suspicions in a huge aria with much coloratura. Mitridate finally makes himself known to his young son, Farnace, who vainly implores him to give up his project of assassinating Pompeo. Next follows still another unsuccessful approach by Pompeo to Giulia; Scipione once more proposes to resign in Pompeo's favor, but Giulia still hesitates to accept his magnanimous offer. The last scene of the second act plays on a darkened stage. Sesto has been admitted by Harpalia to Isicratea's apartments, but she sternly rejects his wooing and orders him out. Apparently absentmindedly, he forgets to take his sword. In the meantime, however, Mitridate himself has found his way to his wife's abode; from concealment (as usual) he overhears her calling Sesto by name, asking him in effect "haven't you gone yet?"—whereupon of course Mitridate immediately suspects the worst. Harpalia takes it upon herself to call Sesto back. Isicratea threatens to kill herself, Sesto is desperate, and Mitridate resolves the situation by seizing Sesto's sword and killing Harpalia on the spot.

In the first few scenes of Act III this sword causes almost as much trouble as did the broken fragment of a similar weapon which Isolde found in Tristan's wound. When Isicratea shows to Pompeo the sword that killed Harpalia he recognizes it as his son's and—true to the tradition of the stern Roman parent—immediately pronounces sentence of death on Sesto. Sesto, thinking at first that it was Isicratea who had been killed, refuses to explain how his sword came to be in her apartments, but when he learns that the victim was only the slave Harpalia, he offers to die in expiation. At this point Mitridate emerges from his customary concealment and magnanimously urges Pompeo to let Sesto live. Pompeo still refuses until Mitridate finally confesses that it was he who killed Harpalia with Sesto's sword—whereupon Pompeo promptly transfers the death sentence to Mitridate, who still refuses to identify himself. In one more love scene, Scipione at last persuades Giulia to accept Pompeo instead of himself. Meanwhile Mitridate, his wife, and his son agree to share the poison which Pompeo has thoughtfully provided for Mitridate's execution; each demands to be the first to die. Pompeo just happens to overhear this family argument and is so affected by it he interrupts their generous strife, forgives them all, sets them free, and installs Farnace as king of Pontus in succession to Mitridate. Giulia is formally handed over to Pompeo and the opera ends with a long aria by Isicratea in praise of liberty.

The foregoing is not a caricature; it is an exact outline of what happens in the opera of *Pompeo*. If the plot perchance seems ridiculous and wildly improbable, I can only submit that it is not much if any more so than the plots of a good many operas to which we listen without overt ridicule today; the events portrayed, the motives of the protagonists, are no less "true to life" than those in *Don Giovanni, Il trovatore,* or *Götterdämmerung,* for example—not to mention our current films and Broadway musicals. It is only that common standards with respect to what may be called the acceptably improbable in opera vary from age to age and from place to place. Just as Italian audiences of the seventeenth century, having presumably read Tasso and Marino, were prepared to accept the imaginary world of the pastorale as a suitable locale for drama, so equally—no doubt having some notions, however vague and confused, about ancient history—they were quite willing to suspend any latent disbelief as to the actions and motives of the heroes of their own remote past. Moreover, they seem to have had an almost pathetic faith that portrayal of the magnanimous deeds of ancient princes might somehow furnish a good example, an incentive to similar unselfish actions from time to time on the part of their own despotic rulers. In short, it should not require any exceptional exertion of our imaginative faculties to understand how the audiences of Scarlatti's time could find the events and motives portrayed in *Pompeo,* as well as those in hundreds of other Italian operas of the seventeenth and eighteenth centuries, sufficiently credible for all practical purposes of the musical theatre.

In any case, the impression of unreality in this libretto is due not so much to the course of the main action itself as to the artificial construction whereby the movement of the drama, apparently in accordance with a tacit rule, is periodically interrupted by love scenes. The idea appears to be that the audience should enjoy the opera scene by scene and not be concerned about continuity; recurrent sharp contrasts are the main requirement. Most of the love scenes are superfluous and many of them are merely repetitious—the incessant wooing of Isicratea by Sesto and the reiterated disputes between Giulia and Scipione, for example. The cast of ten characters is too large: Caesar and Claudio have nothing important to do and could just as well have been left out. Another odd feature is the way in which Mitridate—who is, in a sense, the hero of the whole action—spends most of his time lurking in concealment, emerging only at critical moments and successfully hiding his identity not only from his family for a long time but also from everybody else right up to the final scene of the opera. The motive of magnanimity is overworked: Pompeo of course reveals himself as the great "magnanimous tyrant" in the final scene, but the effect is weakened because there have been similar though lesser displays of high-mindedness on eight or ten previous occasions, not only by Pompeo himself but also by Scipione, Sesto, Mitridate, and even the boy Farnace.

Undoubtedly *Pompeo* is one of the worst librettos Scarlatti ever undertook to set to music; nevertheless, in this his first *dramma per musica* we find already nearly all the material and formal features that will distinguish his work of that type right up to the last. Here already are the historical personages, the interweaving plots, the pairs of lovers, the disguises, the magnanimous ruler, and the happy ending. Here also is the clear distinction in the libretto between dialogue and monologue, and the corresponding musical distinction of recitative and aria. Still lacking are the pastoral episodes and, more importantly, the comic characters and scenes—which however will come in as soon as we get to Naples. Yet even in *Pompeo* there is a strange foreshadowing of the later comic interludes in the role of the slave Harpalia, the only representative in this opera of the lowest social order. Harpalia is a character of the intriguing servant girl type. She is quite willing to introduce a lover into her mistress' bedroom, to joke with him, and even to listen to a little lovemaking from him on her own account; unfortunately, however, her promising career is cut short at the end of Act II when she is murdered—on stage (a striking contrast to the *bienséances* of French tragedy).

There is one incidental peculiarity about Harpalia's role in this opera: in her first scene, in Act I, she is a soprano; in Act II she appears to be a tenor. Possibly there is a simple explanation: the only surviving score of *Pompeo*, in the Royal Library at Brussels, is not Scarlatti's autograph but a copy; and since, as Croce informs us,[4] the role of Harpalia when the opera was given at Naples in

---

4. Benedetto Croce, *I teatri di Napoli, secolo XV–XVIII* (Naples: L. Pierro, 1891), p. 180: "il Sig. Domenico Gennaro, Musico del Duca di Guadagnuolo."

1684 was sung by a tenor, it seems likely that the scribe of the Brussels manuscript had copied Act I from a Roman source (possibly the autograph) and Act II from a Naples manuscript. Alternatively, of course, the tenor may have sung in falsetto in Act I—a practice not unusual in comic roles.

Although the distinction between aria and recitative is clear in *Pompeo,* there are a number of other features in the score which are present likewise in the contemporary productions of Stradella and Pasquini and which by comparison with Scarlatti's later works can be called definitely conservative—conservative both in that they conform apparently to common practice in Roman operas of the 1670s and '80s and also in that Scarlatti himself in the course of time gradually abandoned these practices or modified them as his style matured. In the first place, the structure of the scenes is not always like that found in the librettos of Scarlatti's later works. There is little trace of the later convention whereby a singer leaves the stage immediately after his aria—the so-called exit aria. Several scenes of *Pompeo,* in fact, end not with an aria but with recitative—for example, the important final scenes of Acts I and II. Moreover, the last act ends with a solo aria instead of the ensemble that later became standard for this place. On the other hand, the respective styles of recitative and aria in *Pompeo* are perfectly distinct; occasionally a recitative at the end will go into a brief melodic arioso passage by way of transition to the following aria, but this practice is not nearly so common in *Pompeo* as it was in *Gli equivoci* and Scarlatti's other early operas. The arioso transition was a heritage from the past—Cavalli, Cesti, and Pasquini frequently introduce it—but already in 1683 it was becoming an anachronism. Scarlatti has very little use for it. His recitative in general is conventional *recitativo semplice* or *secco,* with rapid non-melodic declamation in eighths and sixteenths, with the usual forms of recitative cadences and in addition fairly often the old-fashioned cadence formula (interval of a half-step):

o - no - re

While the majority of the scenes in *Pompeo* consist simply of the normal recitative-plus-aria, there are a number of cases in which this order is reversed. Even more characteristic of this opera is the construction whereby a scene begins and ends with an aria, with recitative between. This structure, to be sure, is still found in many of Scarlatti's later operas, but less frequently than in *Pompeo*. As a general rule, in such cases the opening aria will be comparatively short and simple and the closing aria longer and more elaborate.

Apart from the variable or what may be called the nonstandard construction of many of the scenes, a conspicuously old-fashioned feature of *Pompeo* is the large proportion—fully half the total number—of arias in strophic form: always two strophes musically identical, with a short ritornello (usually for full orchestra) after the first and sometimes also repeated after the second strophe. This form of aria had been a favorite in Italian opera from the beginning and it lasted, though with diminishing frequency, well into the eighteenth century. In its most common type—with a single ritornello between the stanzas—one can view it as obviously an earlier "stage" of the da capo aria, though it seems far less suited to dramatic situations than the later, more highly developed form. Within each strophe the pattern will most often be tripartite with a contrasting middle section (A B A); more rarely, at least in Scarlatti, each strophe will be in the so-called *seicento* form of three parts, the second and third being melodically identical but usually at different pitch levels—first perhaps in the dominant or subdominant and then repeated in the tonic. Among the nonstrophic forms of arias in *Pompeo* the most numerous are those in straight three-part (A B A) form, the direct ancestor of the full da capo aria of the eighteenth century. It is perhaps a curious detail that in the one surviving copy of *Pompeo,* and in the scores of this period generally, the repetition of part A of these three-part arias is almost always written out in full, even though it would certainly have been possible in most cases simply to write "da capo" at the end of the B section and place a fermata over the last note of the A section to indicate the end, as was the later practice. In fact, I suspect this was just what the composers did; the unnecessary writing out of the A section was probably the copyists' idea: after all, if they were paid by the page they had an obvious incentive to produce as many pages as possible. Moreover, the contribution of the copyists in some, perhaps in many, of these operas was more important than we might expect. There are known cases in which the orchestration of the aria accompaniments was due to the copyist rather than to the composer.

An occasional formal feature of *Pompeo,* and of other early operas of Scarlatti, is the use of a persistent short ostinato-bass figure throughout an aria. Arias over a repeated bass pattern are of course found in Italian opera from the very beginning (in Monteverdi's *Orfeo,* for example); the device was fairly common in Venetian operas of the middle to late seventeenth century and is very frequent in Scarlatti's *Honestà negli amori.* With Scarlatti, it is most often a "modulating ostinato," the persistent short bass pattern being repeated in one or more related keys before finally returning to the tonic. Still another detail to be noted in *Pompeo* is the "motto" beginning of many of the arias—the voice as it were announcing the subject of the musical discourse to come, in a single phrase, after which there is a short instrumental phrase on the same motive and then the aria proper begins. If the aria is strophic the initial "motto" phrase will not always be repeated at the beginning of the second strophe. This feature can be found in Scarlatti's operas right up to the last. Commonly the motto consists simply of the opening phrase of the aria itself, but there are also examples in the later operas of a more formal kind of "motto," almost like a proclamation, an announcement that an aria is about to begin, a phrase melodically unrelated to anything in the aria proper and sometimes giving obvious opportunity to the singer to ornament it with vocal embellishments—but devices of this sort belong to a later stage of our survey. The "motto" in *Pompeo* and other Scarlatti operas before 1700 is a much simpler affair.

All the foregoing details of musical forms and patterns may be thought of and included under the most comprehensive dichotomy, namely the division of Scarlatti's opera arias into two fairly distinct categories which we may call for convenience simply "little" and "big" arias—the former being short, with simple melodic lines, few or no harmonic audacities, accompanied by a reduced orchestra or by the continuo only, and occurring at points of relative repose in the action; the "big" arias by contrast being longer, sometimes with more or less elaborate coloratura passages, accompanied typically by the full string orchestra (and in the later operas sometimes with additional wind instruments or exceptional division of the strings), often exploiting special harmonic and melodic progressions, and occurring nearly always at moments of high tension—either in response to sudden catastrophic events in the drama or at a point where one of the personages can appropriately give vent to exceptionally strong feeling in response to the situation then obtaining. With regard to the distribution of the two kinds of arias, it does not matter how important the personage is in the social scale; the biggest persons— kings, for instance—do not necessarily get the biggest arias. The kind of aria depends on the dramatic situation at a given moment and the prevailing principles of alternation and contrast.

Now of course no broad generalization such as this can apply rigidly to a body of material as vast and varied as the total operatic output of a composer like Scarlatti; exceptions to the foregoing description of aria types can always be found. More exceptions can be explained by the well-known necessity that composers were under of providing the right number and the right kinds of arias at the right places for certain singers—especially famous singers —in the cast. But, exceptions aside, the above distinction and descriptions do hold basically for all of Scarlatti's operas, as we shall see.

·*III*·

Naples,
1684–1702

Before following Scarlatti and his family to Naples we may briefly mention more operas which can appropriately be assigned to the composer's first Roman period. Although written in Naples, these were commissioned by Roman patrons, designed for Roman tastes and moreover were conducted in Rome by the composer himself at their first performances.

Such periodic trips to Rome—and there were others besides these—are evidence of Scarlatti's loyalty to his early patrons as well as of his practical sagacity in retaining the valuable Roman connections. Although he is commonly thought of as a Neapolitan composer, and in fact is often regarded as the founder of the "Neapolitan school of opera," it would be almost equally appropriate to think of Scarlatti as a Roman. He began and ended his professional operatic career in Rome, and actually lived there during about half of the most active years of his life. The operas *Rosmene* (1686), *La Rosaura* (1670), and *Statira* (1690)—all designed for Rome and first produced there—while much better in every respect than *Pompeo,* are more nearly akin stylistically to that work than to the operas Scarlatti was producing at Naples in the 1690s. *Rosmene* perhaps has an even earlier connection with Rome: at any rate, there was a little *dramma per musica* performed there in Cardinal Pamphili's palace in 1677 which had three personages with the same names as three of those in *Rosmene*; but since neither score nor libretto nor even the title of this work has survived it is impossible to say whether Scarlatti incorporated any parts of it in his opera of 1686.

Rosmene is certainly one of the best, if not the very best, of Scarlatti's early operas—despite the libretto, which rather resembles that of *Pompeo* and makes very little more sense, but which does provide copiously the kinds of situations for which Scarlatti could write strong arias of well-defined character. As the opera begins, Rosmene (the heroine) is newly married to Pelope, general of the Maecenian armies, who is away on campaign. Rosmene is steadfastly loyal to her husband, fighting off the repeated amorous attentions of both King Linceo and his son Oronte. Pelope, like Mitridate in *Pompeo,* returns secretly and keeps pretty much out of sight, suffering agonies of jealousy until, toward the end of Act III, he is finally convinced of his wife's fidelity. The proceedings are complicated by the queen's page Eurillo who eventually turns out to be a woman, Fidalma, to whom the prince Oronte had formerly been betrothed. There is a comic servant couple, a man Liso (soprano) and a woman Alcea (tenor)—a distribution of voices fairly common in such roles at this period—who have several scenes to themselves.

With *Rosmene* we find quite clearly the distinction previously mentioned between "big" and "little" arias. The prevailing musical pattern is the strophic, with each strophe in A B A form. There are a few nonstrophic arias in this form and a very few in the *"seicento"* form A B B. The "arioso transition" at the end of recitatives is still fairly common, and sometimes even quite elaborate. As regards the musical forms, therefore, *Rosmene* still has much the same characteristics as *Pompeo.* The difference is not in the formal patterns but in the musical content: themes are more strongly individualized and grow more clearly out of the emotional situation to be depicted; the elements of formal structure are perfectly distinct, based on tonal relationships, but the subordinate formal units are often extremely subtle in phraseology.

Gli equivoci in amore overo La Rosaura is a lighter, altogether less pretentious work than *Rosmene.* Scarlatti composed it, evidently on commission, to be performed at a double wedding involving the families of two of his Roman patrons. The title perhaps includes an allusion to his earlier *Equivoci nel sembiante* and the rather small scale of the action as well as the style of the music are closer to that earlier work than to the two large operas *Pompeo* and *Rosmene*. In a class with the latter, however, is *La Statira* (Rome, 1690) which Dent well characterizes as "a very fine example of the grand manner." *Statira* survives in five contemporary (or at least eighteenth-century) copies at Munich, Cambridge (England), Modena, and Dresden, as well as in nineteenth- or early-twentieth-century copies at Brussels and Washington. Evidently *Statira* was never performed outside Rome; at least, there are no known printed librettos from other cities. There does exist, however, the autograph of the libretto, by Scarlatti's patron Cardinal Ottoboni, which is preserved in the Vatican Library. The plot is based on a conflation of two distinct episodes in the life of Alexander the Great. There are, of course, cross-plots involving love affairs, jealousy, impenetrable disguises, and the usual display of magnanimity by everyone, especially in the final scene. Typical also are scenes of violence and scenes with a pastoral setting (one of which, at the end of Act II, is interrupted by an earthquake). There are no specifically comic scenes, but the lower order of society is represented by one male servant, Perinto (soprano). An unusual personage in this opera is Apelles, the most famous painter of antiquity, court painter to Alexander the Great; the opening scene of Act II is a picture gallery with paintings (presumably by Apelles himself) displayed.

The orchestra of *Statira* consists of the usual string band, with the addition of trumpets in Alexander's triumphal scenes. Arias for the most part are in the usual three-part (A B A) form, the repetition being identical with the first part but—as always in the early Scarlatti scores—copied out in full by the scribe instead of being simply indicated by the words "da capo" or "dal segno" as was usually done in the later operas. About half the arias have a second strophe. Three roles in the cast are for sopranos; Statira, the heroine, is an alto; there are two tenor roles and one bass.

By the time of his success with *Pompeo* in 1684 there would seem to have been every reason for Scarlatti to look forward to a successful career at Rome. His patrons were numerous and influential; already he was becoming known throughout northern

Italy and his music was much in demand. He held the proud post of *maestro di cappella* to Queen Christina and had produced at least seven operas and as many oratorios, as well as an unknown number of cantatas, motets, and other smaller works. But there were drawbacks at Rome. Chief among these was the ever-growing attitude of opposition to the theatre on the part of the popes, which resulted eventually in the closing of all public theatres. This atmosphere of official disapproval was discouraging enough in itself for a composer whose main interest was opera. Private patronage was, as always, uncertain in the long run. Scarlatti's principal patron, Queen Christina, however brilliant a figure in Roman society, was not rich, and it must have occurred to her young protégé (though he certainly would never have said so aloud) that, after all, Her Majesty was nearly sixty years old and in the natural course of things could not be expected to be around much longer. And there was still another factor in the situation. According to current rumor in Rome—duly reported in the local gossip columns—one of Scarlatti's sisters had seduced a priest and moreover had actually married him. Whether or not the story was true, it appears to have been believed in the highest quarters; and so to the general official dislike of everything connected with the theatre there was added a particular enmity against the whole Scarlatti family—another motive for young Alessandro to begin looking elsewhere for his future career.

At about this time there sojourned in Rome a certain Neapolitan nobleman, Domenico Marzio Carafa, Ducca di Maddaloni. The duke had heard *Gli equivoci nel sembiante* at its first performance in 1679 and was so impressed by the music that he had the opera performed in his own palace at Naples a year later. Undoubtedly it was Duke Maddaloni who recommended Scarlatti to his good friend the Marchese del Carpio, who in 1679 was the Spanish ambassador at Rome and who four years later became viceroy of Naples. At his invitation, the Roman Scarlattis in 1684 moved to Naples where the remaining members of the family from Palermo soon joined them.

By both geography and history, the kingdom of Naples was something apart from the other states of Italy. Its area comprised nearly all the southern half of the peninsula; much of it is mountainous and its soil in the farming localities is poor.[1] The city of Naples itself is situated, as everyone knows, on one of the most beautiful bays in the world, almost in the shadow of Mount Vesuvius, near the sites of Pompeii and Herculaneum, not far from the grave of Virgil, the cave of the Cumaean sybil, and other places renowned from antiquity. One cannot help feeling that the constant contrast between great natural beauty and the ever-present threats of great natural forces of destruction has had an influence on the psychology of the Neapolitans, an influence extending to their art, literature, music, and even their history. In reading the *Giornali* of Confuorto, that lively hodgepodge of news reports, court circular, society column, and sharp-tongued gossip covering the years 1680 to 1699, one is constantly reminded of three recurring sources of terror in Naples: the menaces of volcanic eruption, of earthquakes, and of the plague. A visitation of the plague in 1656 is said to have carried off half the population of the city, and there was a bad scare in 1690–91, the sickness raging in various towns round about, and Naples itself in a state of terror under strict quarantine. Older people still remembered the great eruption of Vesuvius in 1631, and there were threats of a similar catastrophe in the late 1680s and early 1690s, intensified by a very destructive earthquake in 1688. (Earthquakes, incidentally, occur in at least two of Scarlatti's operas around this time.) Against all such menaces the only defense seems to have been a somewhat tremulous reliance on the power of prayer and trust in holy relics, especially in the miracle of the liquefaction of the blood of the city's patron saint, Januarius, which occurred regularly in May and September of every year. Sometimes the saint was slow in working the miracle and this was considered a bad omen.

The city of Naples and the southern part of Italy generally, as well as the nearby island of Sicily, had for centuries been involved with affairs of the Near East. First colonized by Greek settlers in the eighth century B.C., they had later come under the domination of Carthage and then of Rome. They had been largely overrun by

1. This circumstance is receiving attention just now in connection with efforts to bring the living standards of the region more nearly up to those of the other parts of the country.

the Moslems in the tenth century, though a few enclaves on the mainland still acknowledged the feeble rule of Byzantium. After many wars and revolutions and a period under Norman kings in the eleventh century, southern Italy enjoyed a glorious interlude of peace under the great emperor Frederick II, who founded the University of Naples in 1224. After a period of division, Sicily and Naples were again reunited by Alfonso the Magnanimous, only to be divided on his death in 1458, when Sicily went to the king of Aragon and Naples was left under the rule of Ferrante (or Ferdinand), Alfonso's illegitimate son. But in 1504 the Spaniards conquered Naples, and from then on until the War of the Spanish Succession in the early eighteenth century the kingdom remained virtually a province of Spain and a headquarters of Spanish power in the Italian peninsula, governed by a viceroy as agent of the Spanish king.

On the whole, the 200 years of Spanish rule (1504–ca. 1708) were a time of peace and relative well-being for the kingdom of Naples. The Spaniards were not loved, but they seem to have been endured for the most part with a kind of fatalistic apathy. The only serious outbreak against them was the brief revolt led by Masaniello in 1647. While this episode had no great consequences at the time, it played a curiously indirect role in European history nearly two centuries later. When Auber's opera *La muette de Portici,* the plot of which is based on Masaniello's career, was performed at Brussels in 1830 it touched off a popular uprising that resulted eventually in the constitution of Belgium as an independent state. Meanwhile, the Spanish regime in Naples in the sixteenth and seventeenth centuries was not of a wholly reactionary character. Rather tardily, the last remnants of feudalism disappeared. Under successive viceroys many of the old tyrannical privileges of the barons were abolished, while the commoners and to a certain extent the middle class of people generally came to exercise more control over their own affairs. Naturally, many of the ancient nobility continued to hold on to their titles long after their former wealth and privileges were gone. In the seventeenth century, Croce tells us,[2] there were in Naples "no less than 119

2. Benedetto Croce, *History of the Kingdom of Naples* (1925; Eng. trans. Frances Frenaye, Chicago: University of Chicago Press, 1970), p. 119.

princes, 156 dukes, 173 marquises, and hundreds of counts, with titles that often did not go with a fief but were attached to mere fields and farms"—a situation which of course was a standing joke all over Europe and was sometimes satirized in comedies. Along with all this display of social standing went an extreme regard for fine points of behavior—of the rules of etiquette, correct use of titles, proper precedence in all situations, deference to superiors, and above all an almost pathological sensitiveness to real or imagined affronts. Let anyone inadventently tread on a nobleman's toe, jostle him at the entrance of a theatre, or hold up the passage of his carriage in the street, and in an instant swords would be drawn and blood be shed. Confuorto's diaries are full of such episodes—not all of which, however, seem to have ended fatally. But violence in Naples always lurked under the polished surface of aristocratic behavior, like the threat of earthquake below the lovely surface of the landscape. Torture was a routine technique in police investigations of crime. The numerous scenes of violence and cruelty in Scarlatti's operas are not such exaggerated pictures of everyday realities as one might wish to think. Under the vice-regal administration of Scarlatti's patron the Marchese del Carpio (1683–87) many earlier abuses began to be reformed. Duelling was discouraged, as was also the old habit of arbitrary and cruel treatment of common people by the nobles; women, "formerly segregated in the Spanish manner, were invited into the drawing room to preside over the gentlemen's conversation, and Spanish dress gave way to the new French style."[3]

Naples was at this time the most populous city in Italy, and perhaps in all Europe. By the end of the seventeenth century its inhabitants numbered 186,000; of these, one person in every fifteen was a "religious," that is, a priest, monk, or nun. There were in the city some one hundred monasteries and forty convents, and the intricate tangle of ecclesiastical and secular legal systems made the administration of law a very complicated affair. Naples had always successfully resisted the establishment of courts of the Inquisition within her borders, but the kingdom nevertheless was as secure a Catholic stronghold as Rome itself. Protestants and

3. Ibid., p. 140.

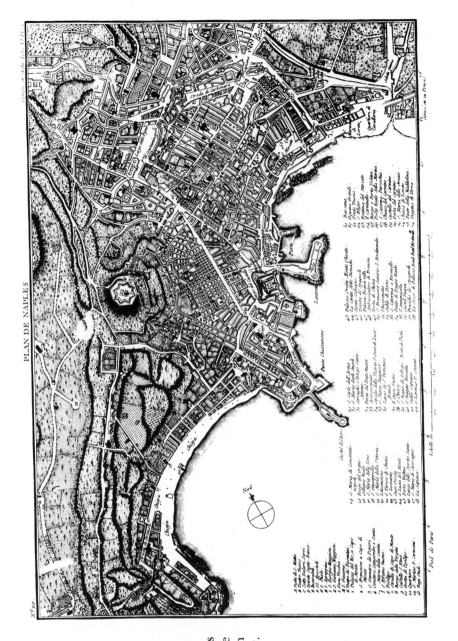

Naples
in the
mid-eighteenth
century.

An opera performance at the Teatro San Bartolomeo in Naples in the eighteenth century.

other heretics were diligently hunted out. It was said that the few English travellers who visited Naples with no more insidious purpose than to enjoy a view of the bay and of Mount Vesuvius tried to disguise their nationality and went about in fear of their lives.

Opera had come to Naples much later than to the northern cities of Italy. The earliest recorded operatic performance was in 1651 when a visiting troupe from Venice (or possibly from Rome) presented a probably altered version of Monteverdi's *Poppea* at the viceregal palace. The principal public theatre was San Bartolomeo, which had been built around 1620 and reconstructed in 1653. From that date there seem to have been fairly regular seasons of opera in Naples. The theatre of San Bartolomeo was completely destroyed by fire in 1688 but was rebuilt two years later and then greatly enlarged in 1696. In addition, the viceroy had a private theatre in his palace and another in his summer residence at Posilippo. New operas as a rule were first given at the palace and then made accessible to the public at San Bartolomeo. The repertoire of the early operas at Naples included works by Cavalli, Cesti, and other Venetians—always with the usual changes and additions by local musicians—but native Neapolitan composers were also represented, notably Francesco Provenzale with his *Schiavo di sua moglie* in 1671 and *Stelladaura vendicante* in 1674.

Scarlatti received his appointment as *maestro di cappella* from the viceroy sometime probably in February 1684, succeeding to the post immediately on the death of the previous incumbent P. A. Ziani. His annual salary was 500 scudi; the two principal singers received respectively 700 and 600 scudi, the other singers 160 to 250 scudi. At the same time Scarlatti's brother Francesco, who had come to Naples as a child some ten or twelve years earlier, was made first violinist of the royal chapel. Trouble broke out at once. Provenzale, who had been honorary head of the chapel since 1680, naturally expected to step into Ziani's post; when the young upstart from Rome was preferred over him, Provenzale promptly resigned and six of the singers left in sympathy with him. A story went the rounds, and was duly reported by Confuorto, that the two brothers owed their appointments to intrigues of one of their sisters—probably not the same one who got Scarlatti into trouble at Rome—with two officials and a "favorite page" of the court. "These" says Confuorto,[4] "made a triumvirate, disposing at their own will of all the usual posts and offices, causing them to be conferred on those who offered the highest prices; and committing other illicit acts to make money and please their theatre drabs—all this without the Viceroy's knowledge, who as soon as he learned of it deprived them of their posts and disgraced them. As for the Scarlatti girl and her companions, he gave order that they should either leave town at once or else retire into a convent; and in conformity with this order they have been placed in the convent of Santo Antoniello." It may be added that the sojourn of these girls within the convent walls was probably not a very long one.

In any case, it would seem that Scarlatti could have had little time in Naples to worry about family affairs. At least two of his operas had already been performed there—*Gli equivoci nel sembiante* privately in 1680 and *Pompeo* at the palace and then at San Bartolomeo in January of 1684, the latter occasion incidentally being notable as one of the earliest triumphs of the famous castrato singer G. F. Grossi, known as "Siface." From the time of his arrival until his departure in 1702, Scarlatti composed, rehearsed, and conducted a total of about seventy operas, an average of nearly four every year. This figure is based on his own statement in a letter of 18 July 1705 to his then patron, Prince Ferdinand de' Medici, in which he says that the opera he was currently preparing for the prince was the eighty-eighth such work he had composed "in less than twenty-three years."[5] Of course he may have been counting among those eighty-eight all the revisions and patchwork, the adding of new arias, new comic scenes, and the like to operas by other composers—from Venice, for example— which he would have been obliged to do as part of his duties at Naples. And of course he may simply have been exaggerating for rhetorical effect. But if he really wrote as many as seventy new operas for Naples in those years, we face the fact (apparently) that almost half those scores have disappeared so utterly that not even

4. Domenico Confuorto, *Giornali di Napoli dal MDCLXXIX al MDCIC,* ed. N. Nicolini (Naples, 1930), 1: 119.
5. Mario Fabbri, *Alessandro Scarlatti e il principe Ferdinando de' Medici* (Florence: L. S. Olschki, 1961).

the titles are known; and of those remaining—those known by title—only about half survive in full score, the rest existing only as librettos or in more or less fragmentary portions of the music, that is, from collections of arias. Still, taking the most conservative figure, a total of forty operas in eighteen years is no mean achievement, though perhaps such a rate of production would not have been so very exceptional in Scarlatti's time. (Think, for example, of Vivaldi's 450 concertos.) In addition, during those years Scarlatti composed at least seven known serenatas, nine oratorios, and sixty-five cantatas—figures again certainly far below the actual totals. And there were those periodic trips to Rome to conduct new operas and keep in touch with his friends and patrons there. Moreover, Scarlatti's position also required him to compose and conduct music for the viceregal chapel and especially for those frequent times when the viceroy held *cappella reale* in his own chapel or in one of the city's churches, and also on occasions of public rejoicing when an eight-voice chorus might take part in the singing of a Te Deum, accompanied by salvos of musketry in the streets and the firing of cannon from the surrounding fortresses.

Since obviously we cannot analyze all forty (or eighty) of the operas Scarlatti wrote for Naples between 1684 and 1702, we shall take as examples four works that apparently represent the best of his achievement during these years. The first is *Pirro e Demetrio,* which had its premiere at the Teatro San Bartolomeo in January of 1694. *Pirro e Demetrio* is the only one of Scarlatti's operas, except *Gli equivoci nel sembiante,* which had what may be called an international success. It was taken up very quickly at Rome, Milan, and Florence and later at Brunswick (in 1696 and again in 1710); it was the only one of Scarlatti's operas to be performed in London during his lifetime. It appeared there in adaptations, with English text, in 1700, with revivals in 1710 and 1717. Even printed excerpts from *Pyrrhus and Demetrius* were published at London in 1709, all with the customary "corrections" by English musicians and including two collections of "aires" arranged respectively for one and two flutes. The plot of *Pirro e Demetrio,* as usual in Scarlatti's operas, centers around historical personages: Pyrrhus, king of Epirus in the third century B.C., and his brother-

in-law Demetrius I, ruler of the neighboring kingdom of Macedonia.[6] In the libretto of Scarlatti's *Pirro e Demetrio,* historical
verisimilitude is limited practically to the names and family relationship of the two protagonists. The story revolves about a situation rather reminiscent of the Tristan–Isolde–King Mark
triangle: Demetrius sends Pyrrhus to obtain for him in marriage
the princess Climene; but the wooing is ambiguous to the point
where the lady thinks she is betrothed not to Demetrius but to
Pyrrhus—who himself more or less intentionally encourages this
misunderstanding. The villain of the plot is a lady, Pyrrhus' sister
Deidamia, who has been in charge of the kingdom of Epirus during her brother's long absence and is decidedly not disposed to
hand it back to him when he returns. She plots with her lover
Mario to have Pyrrhus assassinated, but the plot is discovered and
Deidamia is condemned to death. She repents, attempts suicide,
and her lamentations eventually make such an impression on Demetrius that he obtains her pardon and makes her queen of
Macedonia, magnanimously handing over Climene to Pyrrhus.
There are the usual supernumeraries and complications, including two men who yearn for Deidamia and make love to her from
time to time with varying success. Deidamia's male servant (a
tenor) is the nearest approach to a comic character in this opera,
but he is actually not so much comic as a mere officious fool.
There is a great deal of "marking time," especially in the first part
of Act III, and it is noticeable that Scarlatti's least interesting
music seems to come in just these long, irrelevant, but apparently
obligatory scenes.

The score as a whole is uneven. There is no longer the gravity,
the sense of taking part in serious and important actions, that
prevails (in spite of all the incongruous details) in *Pompeo, Rosmene,* and *Statira.* The events depicted are not felt as significant in
any other way than as background for piquant encounters among
the personages. The music reflects this variety. There is an extraordinary number of very short arias, many of them rather

6. Demetrius seems to have been a favorite character in operas of the eighteenth
century. Metastasio wrote a libretto about him which was set to music by at least
fifteen composers—one of them being a certain Giuseppe Scarlatti (possibly a
nephew of Alessandro).

graceful little tunes in dancelike rhythm (two of them are actually labelled as minuet and *moto di corrente)* and with only continuo or else a very sparse orchestral accompaniment. Where strong affections are involved, arias will be more weighty, sometimes longer and sometimes with larger orchestra, but always with concentration on sharply personal and subjective feelings. In general, it is the principal characters who have arias of this kind; the music for the subordinate personages, even when they are trying to express very serious sentiments, tends to be in a rather neutral vein and often seems quite inappropriate to the words. The prevailing form in arias is the simple da capo; strophic arias are still present, but fewer in proportion to the whole than in the earlier operas. Sometimes (this is not new) in such arias the second strophe will be sung by a different personage, and in one such case (Act III, scene 2) each strophe itself is in a complete (though short) da capo form. Arioso passages are still often mingled with the recitatives and sometimes with arias. There are interesting details of formal treatment. For example, the last scene of Act II begins with an aria for Pirro, "Veder parmi un ombra nera." The mood of solemn menace indicated by the text is mirrored in the accompaniment *(largo)* of heavy reiterated eighth-notes for orchestra of strings, but, according to express direction, "col leuto senza Cembalo." The first stanza, punctuated by a recitativelike phrase toward the end, is followed by an encounter (in recitative) between two plotters who have come separately by stealth to assassinate Pirro but whose designs are foiled by the accident of their getting in each other's way and incidentally making Pirro aware of their presence. They depart, threatening between their teeth to come back and finish their enterprise at some more favorable time. Pirro, once more alone, then repeats his aria, slightly modified in both words and music. The result is an unusual variant on the basic da capo pattern, extended to cover an entire scene.

Certain mannerisms of Scarlatti begin to appear quite often in *Pirro e Demetrio.* (1) The "motto" beginning of an aria was not a new device at Naples; one has the impression sometimes that its purpose was to say to the audience (after a long passage of recitative), "Pay attention now, here comes an aria and this is its subject, this is what it is about," and the repetition of the first phrase was naturally balanced by a similar repetition of the last phrase, saying in effect, "Goodbye, this is it." (2) More markedly than before we now begin to hear certain characteristic melodic inflections toward the close of an aria: not only the lowered second (appropriately resulting in the "Neapolitan sixth" chord) but also the lowered third, bringing a tinge of minor color toward the end of a major tune. Such inflections will come most naturally when there is the slightest hint of sadness or affliction in the text, and emotionally affective words will produce them even in recitatives. The diminished seventh chord, frequent at precadential situations in the later Scarlatti, is not yet common in *Pirro e Demetrio.*[7]

There is as yet no marked uniformity of scene structure. To be sure, thirteen of the forty-three scenes consist of the standard pattern of recitative plus one aria, but an even larger number (seventeen scenes) begin with a recitative and then go on with an alternating series of short arias or duets punctuated by recitatives. Typically, the first scene of each act, and other scenes that come first in a new stage setting, will begin with an aria. Such diversity in the structure of the scenes is in marked contrast to Scarlatti's procedure in his late operas: in *Griselda* (1721), for example, thirty-six of the forty scenes consist simply of opening recitative followed by an aria or less often an ensemble. One has the impression that the variety of scene structure in *Pirro e Demetrio* is one evidence of Scarlatti's and his librettists' tireless endeavors to please the audiences at Naples. These operas were intended not only for aristocratic patrons—persons presumably of some education and with more or less cultivated tastes—but also for popular entertainment in a public theatre. And for popular audiences, then as now, the essential formula was novelty and surprise within a fixed framework of expectation. The same requirement would perhaps account for the many striking but irrelevant episodes in the plots and the many short, catchy tunes.

A typical opera of this period is *Massimo Puppieno,* which

7. This harmony, in one form or another, is mentioned in Gasparini's *L'armonico pratico al cimbalo* (Venice: Bortoli, 1708) as useful "in certain preparations for the cadence [in recitatives] and for the expression of words of sadness" (p. 57), it is "much used by modern composers . . . in expressive passages, chiefly in recitatives" (p. 66).

played at the Teatro San Bartolomeo in the Carnival season of 1695–96. In addition to the libretto printed for that occasion there are two others which indicate that Scarlatti's music was heard again, with the usual changes and substitutions, at Livorno in 1697 and Florence in 1700. Settings by other composers, testified by printed librettos ranging from 1684 to 1729, indicate an unusually long period of popularity for this drama. Scarlatti's only known complete score is preserved in the library at the Abbey of Montecassino.

The plot takes off from the brief career of M. Clodius Puppienus Maximus, a distinguished Roman general of the third century A.D., who after defeating a rebellious army under the deposed emperor Maximinus entered Rome in triumph and reigned, jointly with two others, for three months in the year 238, until he was assassinated in an uprising by the Praetorian guards—a typical fate of emperors in that century of anarchy in the history of ancient Rome. Scarlatti's opera deals only with the success and triumph of Puppienus; against this pseudohistorical background there unfolds a plot involving the usual crisscross love affairs, deceptions, disguises, treachery, and terror. Maximinus, Puppienus's enemy, rather dominates the proceedings both musically and dramatically, and would be a strong candidate for an award as the most repulsive character in all opera—no mean distinction. There is one very good comic bass role, the servant Gilbo, a shrewd fellow with a quality of humor sometimes suggestive of Leporello.

In general the structure of scenes and the musical forms in *Massimo Puppieno* are like those in *Pirro e Demetrio,* except that there are only a few passages of arioso in the recitatives. There are a number of strophic arias, but the da capo is the most frequent aria form in *Massimo Puppieno.* A common type is the very short da capo, with continuo accompaniment and a following short orchestral ritornello; and it is notable that arias of this type tend to occur in pairs. This pairing of short da capo arias (which I have not noticed in other operas of Scarlatti or his contemporaries) is perhaps important as an element of musical form, compensating, as it were, for the brevity of the individual members by incorporating them into larger formal units.

Both the da capo form and the continuo accompaniment in the arias of these Naples operas suggest a picture of the over-worked composer, forced to make as many minutes as possible of music at the cost of as few minutes as possible for getting the notes written down. Nevertheless, when the situations demand exceptional expressive power Scarlatti rises to the occasion. One such example in *Massimo Puppieno* is the soprano aria "Ardo, sospiro" in Act III, scene 2, in which the sentiment of the text is expressed by the languishing 12/8 metre, the minor key (there is only one cadence on a major chord), the constant downward modulations toward the subdominant region, the diminished fourths and the persistent lowered seconds in the melody. The form is freely treated, through-composed, unified by recurrent melodic motives and a three-part key structure, B minor—E minor–A minor—B minor. Equally vivid and dramatic is the scene of Maximinus's suicide with the recitative-soliloquy "Dove sei traditrice" in Act III, scene 17.

With *La caduta de' decemviri* (1697) we come to what is generally regarded as one of the most important operas of Scarlatti's first Neapolitan period. This work has attracted particular attention from the two leading Scarlatti scholars, Dent and Lorenz. It must be said that the general conclusions of these two authorities are inconsistent with each other and even in some respects contradictory, while some of their details are inaccurate. Dent, for example,[8] speaks of a "new element" in the shape of "cloying airs in 12/8 time, all charming and all exactly alike." One may agree or not with the description, but it is certain that "airs" of the kind described are not a "new element" in *La caduta*. There are such arias already in *Pirro e Demetrio* and in *Massimo Puppieno*: it is true, however, that they are much more numerous in *La caduta*. The relation of this type of aria to the dance tunes called *Siciliana* and to other arias so designated in operas and other vocal works of the seventeenth and eighteenth centuries, is not clear; all that they certainly have in common is the triple subdivision of the beat and the characteristic flatted second in the melody. Tunes of the kind Dent is describing seem to have dropped out of favor by the end

8. Edward J. Dent, *Alessandro Scarlatti: His Life and Works* (1905; new ed. by Frank Walker, London: Edward Arnold, 1960), p. 65.

of the century. If we take as the archetype these arias of langorous moods, with slow or moderate tempi, minor key, and flatted second at the cadences, then there is only one such aria in each of the three operas *Eraclea, Laodicea e Berenice,* and the first version of *Tito Sempronio Gracco,* which date respectively from 1700, 1701, and 1702.[9] It is certainly true that these operas, and especially the last two, abound in the kind of music that Dent characterizes as "of that straightforward, square-cut character that one would naturally describe as 'Handelian' . . . the kind of tune to which even a viceregal foot could quite easily beat time." I would only add that to describe some of these tunes as "Handelian" would be no great compliment to Handel. They are the output of an overworked composer, distraught by money troubles, worried about his future and that of his family in a city lately torn by riot and apprehensive of still more serious disturbances consequent on the political situation in Europe and the threat of war over the matter of the Spanish succession. I do not mean to imply that all these late Naples operas of Scarlatti are simply negligible, but only that the proportion of musically "lightweight" arias in them seems to be unusually high.

To return now to *La caduta de' decemviri:* Dent seems to group this work with the other Naples operas of the late 1690s and early 1700s—one of the best of these perhaps, but not differing from the others in any important respect except for the "new element" of the 12/8 tunes (which, as we have seen, was neither new in this work nor especially conspicuous in the immediately following ones); not marking out any new feature of importance for Scarlatti's later works except for the form of the overture (concerning which we shall have more to say presently). Lorenz,[10] on the other hand, regards *Pirro e Demetrio* (1694) as the "end point" of Scarlatti's youthful style of opera and sees *La caduta* as essentially new, no longer "youthful," with no trace of "transition," a work of "highest mastery," to be regarded as the central point for a study of the "Meisteropern." I hope that these divergent views can be ex-

9. *Eraclea:* "Ricordati che io t'amo," in I, 15; *Laodicea:* "Son come un ruscello," in III, 4; *Tito:* "Mi dicono i tuoi lumi," in III, 8.

10. Alfred Lorenz, *Alessandro Scarlatti's Jugendoper* (Augsburg: Benno Filser, 1927), p. 160.

plained, if not reconciled, by a somewhat closer analysis of *La caduta de' decemviri,* with particular attention to these details in which it resembles or differs from Scarlatti's earlier and the later works.

La caduta was first presented at the Teatro San Bartolomeo in December of 1697. There are further printed librettos also for performances at Livorno, Florence, and Siena over the next five years, and a revival is reported at Genoa as late as 1714. The work had nothing like the widespread success of the early Roman operas, or of *Pirro e Demetrio,* from which no fewer than ten printed librettos survive. The contemporary account of the premiere at Naples states that *La caduta de' decemviri* was received "con universale applauso" and sandwiches Scarlatti's name between a compliment to the librettist (Silvio Stampiglia) and a notice that the occasion was graced by the presence of the viceregal couple and "the flower of the ladies and gentlemen of their court."[11]

The libretto is the usual fantasia on the facts of history, starting this time from an episode in the earliest days of the Roman republic. The second board of the Decemvirs (450 B.C.), under the leadership of Appius Claudius, "instituted a most infamous and tyrannical rule." One of their most outrageous acts concerned Virginia, "the beautiful daughter of a plebeian." Appius Claudius, desiring to gain possession of her, made use of his authority as a judge to pronounce her a slave. The father of the maiden, preferring the death of his daughter to her dishonor, killed her with his own hand. Then, "drawing the weapon from her breast, he hastened to the army . . . and, exhibiting the bloody knife, told the story of the outrage. The soldiers rose as a single man and hurried to the city. . . . The situation was so critical that the Decemvirs were forced to resign."[12] These few facts were all that Stampiglia needed to launch into a typical opera plot, involving intrigues, misunderstandings, three pairs of lovers (five sopranos and one tenor) and a comic servant couple. The father (Lucio) stabs his

11. Roberto Pagano and Lino Bianchi, *Alessandro Scarlatti* (Turin: Edizioni RAI, 1972), p. 149.

12. Philip Van Ness Myers, *Ancient History* (Boston: Ginn, 1904), pp. 386–87; from Livy 3. 44–54.

daughter Virginia in the third scene of Act III; two scenes later, of course, we learn that the maiden was only slightly wounded and has made a fast recovery. Appio repents and Lucio magnanimously forgives him. Everyone else gives expression to the most exemplary sentiments, all misunderstandings are cleared up, and the whole cast unites in a brief closing ensemble with declarations of mutual love.

It may be remarked that the last scene, like the last scene in most of Scarlatti's operas, is of comparatively slight musical interest. The unwinding of the plot and the sorting out of the loving couples is accomplished entirely in recitative; one imagines the audience steadily leaving the theatre throughout these anticlimactic finales, once having taken a critical look at the new stage setting which apparently was obligatory by custom at this place.

The course of the drama in *La caduta de' decemviri* involves many of the special kinds of scenes which we have already noted in Scarlatti's earlier operas. To be sure, there is no scene of a particularly pastoral character, but this does not prevent the heroine Virginia from being found asleep at the beginning of scene 5 in Act III. Disguises—as usual, perfectly unsuspected—are featured in two other scenes of the third act. In another familiar type of scene, wicked Appio is haunted by ghosts and by the memory of his evil deeds. Altogether, one may say that the libretto of *La caduta,* both in subject matter and in what may be called the dramatic accessories, is for the most part quite typical of Scarlatti's operas for Naples in the 1690s. There are, however, two novel features which are going to be important for the later operas: the comic servant roles are for bass and soprano, and these characters have scenes to themselves—two in each of the first two acts and one in Act III—scenes which are actually designated by the word "intermezzo" in one of the sources. (It is true that the comic bass doubles, in disguise, as a particularly villainous villain in some of the serious episodes: a blatant dramatic inconsistency which, one would think, must have struck even a Neapolitan audience of 1697.)

The other salient novelty of the score is the form of the overture. Instead of beginning with a portentous slow introduction (which was common practice in the older Venetian operas and which Scarlatti had followed in *Pompeo* and *Rosmene*), the first movement is a lively allegro with an interplay of solo and tutti phrases; then follow a movement in slow triple metre featuring chains of suspensions and a final dancelike movement in 12/8: in short, the formal plan of the so-called Italian overture or *sinfonia* which will be the usual outline of Scarlatti's overtures from now on.

With regard to the structure of the scenes, *La caduta de' decemviri* has moved no nearer than the previous operas to the eventually predominant model of recitative-plus-aria: only sixteen of the forty-three scenes are in this form. A nearly equal number are what may be called composite scenes, beginning as a rule with recitative and continuing with alternating aria (or duet) and recitative; this scheme is typical for the comic scenes, but it occurs in serious ones as well. There is no fixed rule of the so-called exit aria: a singer may exit on recitative, and does not necessarily exit after an aria. Three scenes begin with an aria, five end with a recitative. An aria may be interrupted by recitative and then resumed. The various sections of an aria may be sung by different singers; and so on.

Specific musical patterns are much more nearly uniform than the scene structures. All but three of the sixty-one arias and duets have the conventional da capo form. At the end of part A most of them repeat the concluding phrase and some of them also repeat the opening phrase at this point. It is a conservative trait that so many of the arias have such thin accompaniment. Two-thirds of the arias and duets have either only the continuo or else continuo with a single line of violins *unisoni*. Typically, however, (and this is true also of the earlier operas) an aria accompanied by the continuo will be followed by a short ritornello (four to eight measures) for the full string orchestra. Sometimes these little ritornellos come at the end of a scene or accompany the exit of a personage; otherwise their function seems to be simply to provide a bit of contrast, a moment of punctuation as it were, of fuller sound in the midst of the prevailing thinner texture of the surrounding aria and recitative.

There are some exceptional touches of orchestration in *La caduta:* two solo violins are specified in three of the arias and an obbligato solo violin in addition to the usual strings in one other aria; one accompaniment calls for viola or "violetta" and violoncello, and one for solo violoncello with continuo; another contrasts solo violins against the continuo and orchestral violins *unisoni*; one or two trumpets join the string orchestra in bravura arias of a military sort. The most striking novelty, however, comes in one of the comic scenes where the bass separates the phrases of his recitative by a peculiar short ostinato figure, evidently played by himself doubled by the instruments of the orchestra, on a "colascione," a rather crude "folk" instrument of the lute type with a very long neck (total length up to 6½ feet), two or three strings, and sixteen to twenty-four moveable frets.[13] The played interludes sketch a circle of tonal centers: G (tune), D, a, e, b, f-sharp, D, G (twice). Evidently the colascione in Scarlatti's time was stereotyped as a low-class instrument; the word survives in modern dictionaries with such a connotation, in the expressions *colascionata* (bad poetry) and *poeta di colascione* (a poetaster).

Now as to Dent's "cloying airs in 12/8 time ... all exactly alike": it is true that the score of *La caduta de' decemviri* includes thirteen arias in 12/8 time, but by no stretch of imagination can more than three of them be described as cloying; all three are in minor keys and all three happen to come early in the first act. Most of the other 12/8 arias are obviously *allegro* or *allegro moderato;* the majority of them are in major keys and on the whole they are quite jolly.

To sum up: *La caduta de' decemviri* is neither an instance of decadence nor a sudden revelation of new directions in Scarlatti's operatic style. In the general character of the libretto and the great variety and freedom of scene structures it is fully consistent with the earlier operas; the prevailing thinness of orchestration is also consistent with the past. The almost exclusive predominance

13. See Charles Burney, *The Present State of Music in France and Italy* (London: T. Becket, 1771, 2d. ed., 1773), pp. 297, 310–12; see also James Mitchell, *The Works of Giuseppe Antonio Brescianello* (Ph.D. diss., University of North Carolina, 1962), pp. 7–8.

of the da capo aria is the outcome of a change that had been going on in Scarlatti's operas for the previous ten years. The form of the overture, the occasional novelties in the accompaniments, and the placing and stylization of the comic scenes are the most important really new features of *La caduta* that were destined to be retained in his subsequent operas.

·IV·

The Years of Crisis,
1702–1708

By the end of the 1690s Scarlatti was having trouble at Naples. Family cares were increasing and his salary was being paid so irregularly that in 1699 he had to present a formal petition for payment of arrears. The death of King Charles II of Spain in November 1700 precipitated the War of the Spanish Succession in which armies of the French Bourbons on one side and the Austrian Hapsburgs and their allies on the other kept all of Western Europe in agitation for the next thirteen years. There was no serious fighting in the kingdom of Naples but the city was in turmoil for some time. There had been a nearly successful conspiracy in 1701 to assassinate the viceroy; at about this time a scurrilous poster outside the palace brought forth a public notice offering a reward of 8,000 scudi "for the head of the author," but on the next morning there appeared by the side of this notice another, offering 80,000 scudi for the head of the viceroy.[1] As part of the kingdom of Spain, Naples was naturally involved in the anxieties and uncertainties of the campaigns, and feelings were exacerbated by occupation of the city for several years by the hated French troops. The fate of Naples was eventually settled when in 1707 the last Spanish viceroy was succeeded by an Austrian viceroy; and from then until 1735 Naples remained an appanage of the Austrian crown. Another and more personal source of anxiety for Scarlatti around 1701 was the future of his gifted sixteen-year-old son, Domenico, for whose talents he could see no secure

1. Benedetto Croce, *I teatri di Napoli, secolo XV–XVIII* (Naples: L. Pierro, 1891), p. 219.

future in Naples. In 1702 Alessandro applied for and obtained leave of absence for four months—an absence which eventually extended over six years; his post was declared vacant in October of 1704.

Scarlatti's hopes at this time were centered on a new patron: Prince Ferdinando de' Medici, son of Grand Duke Cosimo III of Tuscany. Ferdinando was one of the most renowned patrons of music in all Italy, though his activities in this direction were sometimes hampered by financial dependence on his bigoted and tightfisted father. He had already promoted a dozen of Scarlatti's operas at different theatres in Tuscany, including *Pirro e Demetrio* at Siena in 1695 and *La caduta de' decemviri* at Livorno in 1699. Scarlatti doubtless hoped for a definite appointment from Prince Ferdinando in 1702, but when this was not forthcoming he left Florence and took up residence in Rome, holding an appointment as assistant *maestro* at the church of Santa Maria Maggiore and placing himself once more under the protection of his former patron Cardinal Ottoboni. But he did not by any means give up hope for a permanent post with Prince Ferdinando. During the next four years he sent to the prince four new operas, as well as a number of psalms, motets, oratorios, cantatas, and madrigals. The letters which passed between Scarlatti and Prince Ferdinando between 1702 and 1706 are of interest not only because they are (with one or two exceptions) apparently the only writings of Scarlatti that have survived, but also because they include—along with the conventional expressions of submission and flattery—a number of observations that give us some insight into his ideas about music and opera as well as his methods of composition.[2] He desires above all things to make his music conform to the wishes of his patrons and the expectations of the audience; he will take inspiration from the libretto, aiming always to suit the music to the emotions expressed in the text while keeping in mind the particular capabilities of each singer in the cast. He urges careful observance of his directions as to dynamics and tempo. "Where I

2. Published in Mario Fabbri, *Alessandro Scarlatti e il principe Ferdinando de' Medici* (Florence: L. S. Olschki, 1961).

have indicated 'grave' I do not mean 'mournful'; where 'andante,' not fast but rather 'airy' [*non presto ma arioso*]; where 'allegro,' not headlong; where 'allegrissimo,' a tempo that will not hurry the singer nor drown the words; where 'andante lento,' in a manner that excludes the pathetic but is rather amorous longing; above all, no gloom or mournfulness [*nessun malanconico*]. . . . I have always had the idea in composing an opera to make the first act like an infant who is just beginning to toddle about with uncertain steps; the second act like an adolescent who walks in a grown manner; and the third act strong and swift like an ardent youth who undertakes triumphantly every new enterprise."

The correspondence with Prince Ferdinando ends with Scarlatti's pathetic "begging letter" dated 18 April 1707 from Urbino, and the cold reply of the prince, enclosing a gift of money and advising the petitioner to seek comfort from Divine Providence in his hard situation.

It is singularly unfortunate that the scores of the four operas which Scarlatti evidently composed with such special care for Prince Ferdinando have completely disappeared, with the exception of a few arias from *Arminio* (1703) and *Turno Aricino* (1704)— and even these evidently belong not to the original operas, but to revised versions which were prepared respectively for Naples in 1714 and Rome in 1720.

However, there is compensation for the otherwise blank operatic years 1704–7: one of the two works which Scarlatti composed for performance at Venice in 1707 was *Mitridate Eupatore,* and of this we fortunately possess three copies, preserved in libraries at Berlin, Paris, and Brussels. *Mitridate* was written for the Teatro Grimani di S. Giovanni Grisostomo, the only one of the seven opera theatres at Venice that occasionally presented works of the kind designated *tragedia per musica,* and *Mitridate* is the only one of Scarlatti's surviving operas that is so designated. It is laid out in five acts instead of the usual three, and the whole construction suggests a possible influence from Racine's *Mithridate.* The librettist, Girolamo Frigimelica-Roberti, explains that he has taken as the plan of his drama the type which Aristotle calls the plot "with a double story . . . and an opposite issue for the good and the bad personages";[3] in other words, a plot in which the bad people move from a state of happiness to a state of misery while the good people move from a state of misery to one of happiness. This kind of plot, he says, is the one most acceptable to theatre audiences of all countries. Frigimelica-Roberti refers specifically to three Greek dramas, the *Chöephoroe* of Aeschylus and the *Electra* plays of Sophocles and Euripides and adds that, following the example of Zeuxis, he has taken from his originals "Da chi una parte, e da chi un'altro." He then goes on to mention the following parallels:

Mitridate[4]—Orestes
Issicratea—Pylades(Antigono)
Laodice—Electra
Farnace—Aegisthus
Stratonica—Clytemnestra
Nicomede—Mycenian peasant

At the beginning of the opera Mitridate and Issicratea-Antigono have returned to Pontus from enforced exile in Egypt and are about to seek an interview, in their character as Egyptian ambassadors, with the usurping King Farnace. Their aim, of course, is to get rid of him and assume their rightful places as king and queen of Pontus. In pursuit of this design, they make an offer to Farnace and Stratonica to hand over Eupatore to them, either alive or dead as preferred. Stratonica hesitates but Farnace quickly accepts the offer and opts for the victim dead. The supposed ambassadors agree to deliver the head of Eupatore, but insist that "the people" also be present and give their assent. Farnace is surprised at this demand, but agrees. In a solemn ceremony Farnace and Stratonica swear before the gods that they are acting in truth and with pure intentions; but Farnace orders

3. Aristotle, *Poetics* 145a, 31.
4. The historical Mithridates VI (or IV) Eupatore, called the Great, was a famous figure of romance in ancient literature. He was said to be able to converse in twenty-two different languages and to have so inoculated himself that he was immune to poisons. (There is a passing reference to this in Dumas' *Count of Monte Cristo*.) After his defeat by Pompey in 64 B.C. Mithridates committed suicide—being obliged to request a soldier to stab him when poison proved ineffectual—and was buried in the royal sepulchre at Sinope.

Pelopida nevertheless to have the troops on hand when the "ambassadors" return. Meanwhile, Laodice has gotten wind of the deal; not recognizing her brother, and thinking that the supposed ambassadors are about to kill Mitridate, she and Nicomede rouse a band of peasants who detain the two strangers until finally Mitridate persuades Laodice to let him go to the ships (the supposed Antigono remaining behind as a hostage) and bring back proof of their good faith. Mitridate returns from the ships with an urn supposed to contain the head of Mitridate. Laodice is in despair until her brother finally convinces her and Nicomede of his true identity, whereupon they all agree on a course of procedure. (It is noticeable that all this time Mitridate on the one side and Stratonica on the other have scruples and hesitate, but both are forced on—Stratonica by her husband, Mitridate by his sister.) Mitridate shows the "head" to Farnace, who has an instant of premature rejoicing before Mitridate kills him. They then confront Stratonica with the supposed head, on a platter covered by a cloth. Stratonica after some hesitation removes the cloth and is horror-struck to find that it covered the head not of Mitridate but of her guilty husband and accomplice, Farnace. She requests Mitridate to kill her; while he hesitates, his wife Antigono-Issicratea does the deed. In a big closing scene before the palace, with soldiers and all the people present and rejoicing, the head of Farnace is carried in on a lance. Mitridate is crowned king of Pontus, regrets he had to murder his mother, pardons all domestic enemies, and vows eternal hatred of Rome. (Incidentally, this is the same historical Mitridate whose armies were defeated by the Romans under Pompey in 62 B.C. We have already made his acquaintance in Scarlatti's *Pompeo*.)

The indicated parallels with the personages of Greek tragedy are obvious. The whole libretto reads strangely like the *Electra* of Sophocles. The basic plot motifs are identical: return of the wronged son and rightful heir to the kingdom; recognition by the oppressed sister, revenge and murder of the evil parents. In some details the libretto diverges from the ancient models—for example, in the twice repeated display of the head, the temporary holding captive of Mitridate and Antigono by Laodice, and the killing of Stratonica and Farnace onstage rather than off, as would have been done at Athens. A more important divergence is the killing of Stratonica by Issicratea instead of by Mitridate himself— thereby making Issicratea (Pylades) alone guilty of this murder. There are no allegorical figures corresponding to the Furies of Greek drama. There is a "chorus," but it has nothing like the function of the chorus in ancient tragedy: it is present in this opera only to fill the stage, to be seen, not to be heard. The chorus has nothing to sing except a negligible ten measures in Act III— and so strong is the tradition by now that even this insignificant piece is put in da capo form! Perhaps unique among Scarlatti's operas, *Mitridate* has no love interest, no lovers' quarrels, no pairing off of happy couples in the final scene. Also nearly unique, it has no "magnanimous tyrant": indeed, the sentiment of magnanimity is conspicuously lacking in this drama from beginning to end. Finally, there are no comic characters or comic scenes; the only shadow of a comic role is Pelopida's, but he is really nothing more than a vulgar little one-cylinder villain with not a trace of laughter about him.

One curious feature of this libretto is the rather frequent surfacing of political doctrines, something which doubtless would have been, if not inconceivable, at least very unlikely in an opera intended for Naples. Thus Mitridate demands that the people be present at his coming confrontation with Farnace ("Non t'adular, Monarca / L'universal volere è il tuo Sovrano.") Laodice vehemently exhorts Nicomede to arm the peasants and raise them in revolt against Farnace (Act III, scene 5); she calls in a "stuolo di villani" to threaten Mitridate when she (before recognizing him) suspects him of bad faith (III, 7); and in the final scene the united army and people hail the triumph of Mitridate and accept him as their king. The opposite viewpoint, of course, is represented by Farnace and Stratonica, and their stooge, Pelopida: "mobile è il volgo," "the clever tyrant gives the name of virtue to all the vices of his reign" (III, 4). Farnace: "it is a bad idea to call in foreign armies" (V, 8); "in politics, the masterstroke is sudden surprise . . . when the vulgar rise in arms, the way to deal with them is to strike them with sudden fear" (V, 2). It seems that maxims like these did not die out with Farnace.

The layout in five acts is unique among Scarlatti's surviving operas, but the differences from the usual three-act format are only superficial. There are two different stage settings in each act, plus the usual concluding display scene at the end of Act V. Settings are obviously planned for the maximum of variety and contrast—pastoral backgrounds alternating with courtly spectacles, episodes of rapid action with relatively static interludes, and scenes for only two or three persons with crowd scenes on a full stage.

Turning now to the music we may note first of all that *Mitridate Eupatore* brings to a culmination a tendency which has been increasingly evident in all of Scarlatti's operas hitherto and which will be standard from now on: the organization of each scene in the simple form of recitative-plus-aria. Thirty-one of the thirty-eight scenes of *Mitridate* are in this pattern; only one scene begins with an aria and only one ends with a recitative, and only once do two arias occur in succession. There are three duets, and a rather perfunctory quartet at the end. More remarkable in this opera is the device of opening a scene with an orchestral sinfonia: the first scenes of Acts III and IV begin in this way, and also the sixth scene of Act I, which coincides with a change of décor. The opening of Act IV is a particularly good example of a big display scene; the stage directions read:

> Seacoast, with all the Egyptian warships ranged in good order for the disembarkation. Eupatore descends with great ceremony but with an air of marked sadness, followed by one of his captains carrying a small burial urn. Pelopida advances with attendants and guards to receive it in the name of the King and Queen.

The ceremony is accompanied by a D-major sinfonia in two movements, Adagio-Allegro, the latter featuring two trumpets and tympani on shipboard, answered antiphonally by a similar group in the orchestra plus the full complement of strings and continuo. Disembarkation scenes of this sort are not uncommon in Scarlatti's operas (there are notable ones in *Eraclea* and *Telemaco*, for example). It may strike us as strange that neither these nor similar ceremonial full-stage displays as a rule include a chorus; but the resources of Italian opera houses at this time evidently did not extend to this additional expense. Big scenes of this sort had to be put across therefore with masses, movement, and color onstage, with only the festive sound of trumpets and tympani to help create the desired atmosphere. Another curious detail of this particular scene in *Mitridate* is the way in which the antiphonal effect of the trumpets is accentuated by the direction *alla sordina* for the trumpets in the orchestra.

There are many other interesting details of orchestration in this score. The sheer variety of the aria accompaniments is especially remarkable. When we think about Italian operas of the early eighteenth century we think, naturally, of a succession of alternating recitatives and solo arias all in da capo form; the matter of the accompaniments to the arias is apt to escape our attention, as it no doubt escaped the attention of contemporary audiences. But we need to remember that this seeming monotony of aria after aria is in practice alleviated by the way in which the librettists took care to see that the same singer should not be heard twice in succession, and the composers (or at least Scarlatti) to furnish different orchestral colors as backgrounds for the vocal lines. This is the case with all of Scarlatti's operas except the very early ones, but it is especially notable in *Mitridate* and in some of his later scores. What one may call the standard accompaniment in *Mitridate* is all the violins in unison, plus the continuo; only three short arias in the whole opera are accompanied by the continuo alone and those have the usual short orchestral ritornello at the end. But this standard *unisoni*-continuo texture is often varied by the addition of obbligato solo instruments with their own independent melodic lines: solo oboe (three examples), solo trumpet, solo violin, two solo violoncellos, and combinations of others. The accompaniment of violins I and II and violas over continuo, which is the most common texture in the later operas, occurs only three times in *Mitridate;* but more remarkable in this opera is a richer accompanimental texture of violins I and II, violas, and violoncellos— that is, the complete orchestral string band in four independent parts over continuo. This combination occurs in the sinfonia and in four arias, two of which are especially notable for other reasons as well.

When we think of an opera by Scarlatti (or any other Italian composer of the 18th century) as consisting of an invariable suc-

cession of recitatives and da capo arias, we are perhaps too prone
to conclude that the total effect must be one of deadly uniformity
and hence monotony; but of course this is no more accurate than
thinking all classical symphonies sound alike because they are in
four (or three) movements in a standard order and having more
or less fixed tonal relationships both among the movements and
within each individual movement. It is true that there are certain
internal relationships that are standard for da capo arias and we
may recall these now: the distinct two sections, each with a certain
pattern of harmonic movement about a given tonal center, and the
two sections being in a certain relationship as to length (part B
being shorter) and tonal movement (part B modulating rather
widely and finally cadencing on either the dominant or the minor
mediant of part A). This is the pattern of Scarlatti's da capo arias,
just as the number of movements, their relationships and their
internal structure constitute the pattern of Haydn's symphonies.
But the pattern is only the container; it is the contents that interest us.

Within the pattern of Scarlatti's da capo arias we find a multitude of harmonic, melodic, formal and coloristic details—some
of them obviously responding to suggestions in the text, others
apparently rising out of sheer exuberance of musical invention.
Some of these details in the music of *Mitridate* are:

1. The diversity of orchestral accompaniments. To the instances already mentioned may be added the elaborate solo violin
part in Stratonica's aria "Esci omai" in Act III, scene 3; the coquet-
tish back-and-forth exchanges between solo violin and voices in
the duet at the end of Act III; or the spare but effective "duo"
texture in Eupatore's aria "Chi far gode ad altri frode" in Act V,
scene 1, where the voice is accompanied throughout simply by the
violins *unisoni* making a two-part texture, with the continuo enter-
ing only at the ritornellos. This last is an excellent example of a
"risoluto" aria, with exceptionally clear formal outlines.

2. The significance of certain rhythmic patterns. In Scarlatti's
music, as in that of other composers of his time, each composition
(in this case, each aria) embodies one "basic affection" the funda-
mental expression of which is the rhythm. Without attempting to
pursue this connection in a general discussion of musical aesthe-

tics, we may point out some specific instances in *Mitridate* where rhythm is one factor in establishing the connection between the idea of the text and the character of the music that embodies that idea. Thus in Act II, scene 1 we have a solemn moment when Mitridate and Issicratea-Antigono, having been ceremoniously received at the court of their enemies, the usurpers Farnace and Stratonica, find themselves alone, ready to begin their desperate project of vengeance on the usurpers and restoration of themselves as rightful rulers of the kingdom. Mitridate invokes the aid of the gods in an aria "Patrii numi," with accompaniment in the solemn rhythm of dotted eighths and sixteenths (see example 3).

3. Coloratura, expressive or decorative. In general, extended vocal coloratura passages in Scarlatti tend to come toward the end of part A and (less extended ones) at the end of part B of an aria. Formally, therefore, their function is to accentuate the main climactic points of the aria. Coloratura is most often heard in arias of comparatively light, carefree expression, but there are also coloratura passages of a more serious, vehement nature, associated usually with moods of anger, defiance, strong resolution, and the like. Such is the coloratura at the end of part A of Laodice's aria "Se il tuo sdegno" in Act I, scene 6 of *Mitridate*. Laodice has just reproached Stratonica with her crimes: hatred, deception, murder, adultery, incest; Stratonica threatens to have Laodice killed and handed over to the Furies of the underworld. Laodice defies her in an aria in G minor, *a tempo giusto*, with orchestral accompaniment of unison violins and continuo. The stark texture of this aria consists for the most part of only two lines, voice against violins which play in octaves with the continuo bass. Laodice is saying "If your anger and my destiny will that I should die, so be it; but I will have revenge, I will make you envy my fate"—"con l'invidia di mia morte l'onta almen vendicherò"—and the main climax of the aria, at the end of part A, is emphasized by a long, obviously one-breath coloratura on the word "vendicherò."

One of the finest big coloratura arias in this opera comes in the third scene of Act III. Farnace and Stratonica have just concluded their infamous bargain with the supposed Egyptian ambassadors, in a huge crowd scene where Mitridate solemnly vows before the gods to deliver the head to the usurper. Stratonica, inwardly distrustful and with an uneasy conscience because of the treachery about to be consummated, tries to reassure both her husband and herself that she is really wholeheartedly in favor of the plan that involves her son's death. "Esci omai," she says: "Depart, O motherly love, for there is no longer room for you in my bosom; a more worthy flame burns in this royal heart, the flame of desire for the public good." It is the old Roman maxim of the Twelve Tables: *Salus publica suprema lex esto,* "let the public good be the highest law," and Stratonica with full awareness is about to condone a horrible crime in obedience to this political maxim. Scarlatti has dealt most conscientiously with the text: a long orchestral introduction ending with a quasi-recitative passage, *adagio,* for solo violin (already mentioned), suggest the conflicting emotions in Stratonica's mind. She sings boldly of her high resolve, affirming her resolution in a vigorous climactic passage of coloratura— but immediately the sober repeated full chords of the orchestra suggest the doubt that is troubling her. Stratonica's further words (the second part of the aria) again affirm her resolution—but now she begins in a minor key and ends with an *adagio* cadence and the same full chords of doubt. This is a da capo aria, so presumably the entire long introduction is heard again before the repetition of the first part of the aria. A later composer would no doubt have dealt quite differently with a text of repressed conflicting emotions like this, but the da capo convention was so firmly fixed that it probably never even occurred to Scarlatti to depart from it. Yet in spite of the seeming handicap of this pattern—in other words, within the framework of an established form—Scarlatti has admirably depicted the complex emotional situation involved (see example 4).

Mitridate Eupatore, after one season at Venice in 1707, was revived at Milan ten years later. This seems to have been the extent of its popular success in Scarlatti's day, though it has had a number of revivals in modern times.[5] How are we to account for the comparative failure of *Mitridate* at Venice? In part it may have been due to the unusual nature of the libretto; but it seems to

5. Among them one by the Bel Canto Opera Company at New York in March 1975.

have been due also to simple personal dislike of this "know-it-all foreigner" who evidently did not comport himself with becoming deference toward the bright young Venetian critics of the day. We get this impression from a rather nauseating contemporary satirical poem by one Bartolomeo Dotti, [6] who combines malicious allusions to scandals involving the women opera singers with observations whose tendency appears to be that there is so much "noise" in the music of *Mitridate* that no one can hear what is going on. Insofar as this means anything at all, it probably reflects the growing preference in Italy at this time for a style of opera in which everything is to be sacrificed to attractive vocal melodies without the burden of "counterpoint"—a then fashionable pejorative word for anything in a musical texture that might conceivably detract from unalloyed enjoyment of a tune. When the young Handel presented his *Agrippina* at Venice in 1709, two years after *Mitridate*, he apparently had "gotten the message." That score on the whole is more transparent than Scarlatti's: Handel tends to save his "counterpoint" for the introductions and interludes of arias; during the singing, the orchestra retires discreetly to the background, so that the audience seldom has more than one melodic strand to attend to at a time. *Agrippina* is a beautiful opera, undoubtedly a work of genius. It is evident that Handel, during his Italian years and his friendship with Domenico, had absorbed much from the example of Alessandro; but as a younger man he was more sensitive to the demands of changing modern taste in opera music and hence better able to please the exacting public of Venice.

After the disappointment at Venice Scarlatti returned to Rome, sojourning on the way from April to September at Urbino where his eldest son, Pietro, was *maestro di cappella* at the cathedral. It would be interesting to know what Alessandro was doing during these five months, but apparently no documents exist except for manuscripts of a couple of cantatas dated September 1707.

The situation at Rome was difficult and unsatisfying. Scarlatti

6. Reported in Andrea Della Corte, ed., *Satire e grotteschi* (Turin, 1946), pp. 243–48; also in Roberto Pagano and Lino Bianchi, *Alessandro Scarlatti* (Turin: Edizioni RAI, 1972), pp. 184–89.

already in 1705 had written to his patron Prince Ferdinando that "Rome has no roof to shelter music, which lives here like a beggar." The complaint was certainly, and for obvious reasons, exaggerated, but it did accurately reflect the situation as far as opera was concerned. All public theatres had been closed since 1700. Scarlatti's output for Rome during these years consisted chiefly of serenatas, cantatas, oratorios, and motets. In 1706 he was elected, along with Corelli and Pasquini, to membership in the famous academy called the Arcadia, the foundation of which dated from the days of Queen Christina—an honor which no doubt brought satisfaction but certainly no additional income. In spite of his advancement in 1707 to the post of *maestro di cappella* at the church of Santa Maria Maggiore, his financial situation seems to have grown steadily worse, as his letter to Prince Ferdinando in that year so pathetically discloses. Apparently also there was some difficulty with his Roman patron Cardinal Ottoboni, to which he alludes with great reserve in that same letter. After some preliminary negotiations Scarlatti in 1709 accepted the invitation of Cardinal Grimani, the new Austrian viceroy of Naples, to return to that city, assuming his former post as *maestro di cappella* to the viceregal court.

$\cdot\mathcal{V}\cdot$

Naples and Rome,
1709–1721

WHEN SCARLATTI RETURNED to Naples, late in 1708 or at the beginning of 1709, he entered on a situation which seems to have
been considerably more favorable than that to which he had been
subject during his earlier period of service to the viceroys. No
longer, apparently, was he forced to supply two or even three new
operas for each season; his known operatic productions for Naples
over the next ten years come to a total of eleven, plus two works
he wrote for Rome during this same period. He was relieved, at
least to some extent, of his former chores of revising the music
and composing additional scenes for operas by other composers
for the Naples stage. Scarlatti, by now forty-eight years old, after
the distresses of the past few years could begin to feel himself
relatively secure, with the prestige of an established reputation
and in an environment on the whole favorable to good work.
Moreover, he undoubtedly welcomed the opportunity to return to
his favorite medium of opera. We can discern in these late operas
a more assured style than in the early works. There is an un-
diminished fertility of ideas together with a new feeling of
amplitude and variety. The da capo aria is still the mainstay; the
dimensions of the arias if measured by stopwatch are not very
much greater than in the early operas, but they seem larger because they are internally more varied and also because of a now
perfected tension, a classic balance between the two poles of spon-
taneity of invention on the one hand and an accepted canon of
form on the other. There is also another kind of tension in these
arias, namely that between the tune and the bass. It was this essen-

tially contrapuntal texture which, probably more than anything else, caused Scarlatti's music to be regarded as old-fashioned by Bartolomeo Dotti and other progressive young critics of the day.

La principessa fedele (San Bartolomeo, February 1710) is one of the most melodious and most romantic of Scarlatti's *drammi per musica*. The original libretto, by Agostino Piovene, had been set to music by C. F. Gasparini and performed at Venice in the autumn of the previous year. It is a rescue opera with a plot strikingly similar to that of *Fidelio*. The theme of the heroic wife had been common to both folklore and literature long before Scarlatti; the oriental setting of *La principessa fedele,* however, was more of a novelty in 1710, though there had been a few earlier examples in opera and were to be many more in the course of the eighteenth century, especially after 1740. The most famous of these, of course, is Mozart's *Entführung* which, like *La principessa fedele,* combines the rescue motive with the oriental scene in a plot enlivened by touches of comedy.

Two important changes had to be made in Piovene's libretto for the Naples production. One, naturally, was the addition of comic scenes. The anonymous arranger of the libretto for Scarlatti added to the cast a pair of comic servants, giving them several long scenes to themselves and also allowing them to intervene at many opportune (and inopportune) moments in the principal action. These comic roles were sung by a woman contralto, Santa Marchesini, and a bass, Giambattista Cavana, both of whom were among the most famous singers of Italy. With these two stars in the cast it was only natural that the comic element in the Naples *Principessa fedele* should be more conspicuous than was usual even for that city. Another addition to the original libretto affected the ending of the opera: this was the insertion for Naples of a final scene featuring the "benevolent despot," a character whom we have already met several times in Scarlatti's operas. This sudden and unmotivated about-face by a personage who throughout the whole opera had been conducting himself like a particularly shabby sort of villain seems to have disturbed no one at Naples. What apparently did bother them was the alleged difficulty of Scarlatti's music: "too contrapuntal," as one critic puts it, and consequently above the heads of theatre audiences who would have preferred "roba allegra e saltarelli come fanno a Venezia" ("lively stuff and dances like they do at Venice"). Such criticisms seem to have had little or no effect on Scarlatti's successful career at Naples over the next ten years.

There is, however, a curious break in the rhythm of his normal steady production of operas, a break spanning the years from 1710 to 1714. Apparently his only new opera during these four years was *Il Ciro*, a *dramma per musica* which was written not for the viceroy at Naples but for his old patron Cardinal Ottoboni, under whose auspices it was performed at Rome in 1712. There has recently been some conjecture that Scarlatti about this time was experimenting in the then new genre of comic opera in Neapolitan dialect,[1] though no musical examples of such experiments seem to have survived. The year 1712 was also that of the well-known interchange of cantatas between Scarlatti and Gasparini including the former's famous cantata *In idea inhumana*, with the heading "in idea inhumana ma in regolato Cromatico, non è per ogni Professore."

Since the composer was not present for the performances of *Il Ciro* at Rome, the score naturally has somewhat more detailed directions than usual to the players and singers. It is remarkable also in other respects: the number of dance movements, for example—eight in all, though most of them are extremely short ("curious little scraps of music," Dent calls them)[2]—and the unusually large number of accompanied recitatives, eight altogether. There are no comic scenes, but there is one very exceptionally noncomic role for a bass, the shepherd Mitridate (no relation to our former acquaintances of this name). Also remarkable in this score are some particularly grand "effects," especially a great sacrificial scene (I, 13) with marches and choruses.

The Carnival season of 1713 at Naples saw the premiere of *Tigrane,* one of the most successful of Scarlatti's late operas. The occasion brought forth an unusually long and favorable notice in the *Avvisi di Napoli,* which read in part:

1. Roberto Pagano and Lino Bianchi, *Alessandro Scarlatti* (Turin: Edizioni RAI, 1972), pp. 210–14.

2. Edward J. Dent, *Alessandro Scarlatti: His Life and Works* (1905; new ed. by Frank Walker, London: Edward Arnold, 1960), p. 120.

This was the 106th opera of the eminent First Master of the Royal Chapel, Alessandro Scarlatti, whose works have been received with inexpressible praise both here in Naples and in all the principal cities of Italy. There was a very large audience and the success was extraordinary, with praise for the music, the costumes, the scenery, and the variety of the settings. The singers made an especially fine impression. His Excellency the Viceroy was not present, on account of the cold weather.[3]

For once a contemporary newspaper review of a first performance hit the target. There can be no doubt that *Tigrane* is one of the greatest, if not the very greatest, of Scarlatti's operas. Dent's criticisms of the "utter unreality" of the plot and the "outrageous incongruities of the comic scenes" are beside the point, no more relevant to *Tigrane* than they would be to *Die Zauberflöte;* more relevant is his appreciation of the "variety of expression, brilliant coloratura and melodic beauty" of the music.[4] *Tigrane* is one of the very few Scarlatti operas that have been heard in more than one revival in the present century. It is an outstanding example of the way in which a very tight, hidebound art form can be, as it were, expanded from within—the basic structural unit of the da capo aria expanded by means of varied orchestral colors, variety in dimensions, variety and fineness of detail in the musical substance, and above all greater accuracy of expression; the recitative similarly by greater accuracy of expression and by increased use of the *accompagnato;* and, incidentally to these, the continued or expanded use of the "extra" elements of scenic display and spectacle. This was the true line of evolution of Scarlatti's style; because it did not coincide with the progress of operatic style in Italy generally in the eighteenth century, Scarlatti's operas marked a final stage in the evolution of a species. *Tigrane* is thus a late work in more senses than one.

A special place in the list of Scarlatti's operas must be held for *Il trionfo dell'onore* of 1718, which is called on the title page of the libretto a *commedia* instead of the common designation *dramma*. It was presented in Naples not at San Bartolomeo but at the smaller

3. On the second evening the crowd was so great that extra chairs had to be brought in. Quotation from the *Avvisi di Napoli* in Carl Reginald Morey, "The Late Operas of Alessandro Scarlatti" (Ph.D. diss., Indiana University, 1965), pp. 102–3.

4. Dent, *Alessandro Scarlatti*, p. 125.

Teatro dei Fiorentini, which had started in the early years of the century simply as a rival to San Bartolomeo but which by 1714 had begun to specialize in comic operas. Here we must make some distinctions and clarify terms. There were three kinds of comic operas in Naples at this time: (1) low-class popular comedies typically in Neapolitan dialect, with music mostly by obscure composers, these early examples being quite unpretentious and short-lived pieces, very few of which have been preserved. So far as the record goes, Scarlatti wrote no comic operas of this type—or if he did, he doubtless regarded them as beneath the dignity of a vice-regal *maestro di cappella* and took care to see that no traces of his authorship remained. It was only later, at the hands of Vinci and Pergolesi, that this genre came into its own. (2) The intermezzi, which historically originated from the comic scenes of regular opera and later in the century cut loose from that connection to lead a life of their own. Scarlatti himself had provided two of the three intermezzi of this sort for Lotti's *Giove in Arco* (Dresden, 1717) and had also written intermezzi for his own *Teodora Augusta* of 1692 and for at least three other operas of his in 1714 and 1716. These later intermezzi evidently enjoyed some degree of popularity, since apparently they were revived for production at Venice and Bologna as late as 1724 and 1730 respectively. (3) The third genre was the *commedia in musica,* operas on comic librettos whose origins go back to the Spanish comedy of the seventeenth century, and whose musical structure of alternating arias and recitatives differs in no formal respects from that of an ordinary opera. It is to this third type that Scarlatti's *Trionfo dell'onore* (on a libretto by F. A. Tullio) belongs.

The action is a lively tangle of intrigues and amorous adventures, involving three pairs of lovers and having some resemblances to the plot of Da Ponte's *Don Giovanni,* except that at the end the hero repents and everything turns out happily. Scarlatti's setting is, as regards externals, like that of all his other operas of this period; for example, the practice of constructing each scene as recitative plus aria or duet or other ensemble, is by now firmly established. Nearly every scene in *Il trionfo dell'onore* (except, of course, those scenes that consist only of recitative) is in this form, the only exception being the opening scenes of Acts I and II and the finales of Acts I and III. But within this rigid framework there are certain modifications of detail calculated to adapt the conventional form to a comedy plot. One noticeable peculiarity of this score is the excessive number of scenes in each of the first two acts—respectively twenty-six and thirty-one as against the normal average of fifteen to eighteen for a *dramma per musica;* but since a new "scene" in an Italian opera of this time means not a change of décor but only that someone has left the stage or someone has entered, the large number of scenes in *Il trionfo dell'onore* only reflects the greater bustle of coming and going among the personages, the swifter rate of hither-and-thither turns in the plot, appropriate to comedy as against the more sedate pace of action in a serious *dramma.* Related to this detail is another, namely the exceptional number and length of the recitatives in *Il trionfo dell'onore*—page after page of them in the score, and even these do not reflect the whole quantity of recitative in the libretto, since an unusually large number of lines in the latter are "virgolated"[5] and were never set to music at all.

One of the three lover-pairs in the cast is a comic couple, the traditional old man and old woman; but in addition there are *scene buffe* for a servant pair (contralto and bass) who as usual take part in action with the other personages besides having two big scenes to themselves, one of which forms the finale to Act I while the other occurs near the end of Act II. Both scenes are in the customary form of one or two solos plus a duet, the whole interspersed with recitatives. The other two act finales are ensembles: a quartet at the end of Act II and a brief "octet" at the end of Act III, which however turns out to be only a quartet with two singers on each part. Altogether the score contains five duets and two quartets, plus the pseudooctet at the end: a somewhat larger number of ensembles than might be expected in a serious *dramma.* One looks hopefully but in vain through these ensembles, especially the quartets, for some differentiation of the individual characters such as we are accustomed to find in the ensembles of Mozart. But the time for such clear distinction of the individual within the group has not yet come. It is true that Scarlatti does, in

5. Marked with a double comma at the beginning of each line to indicate omission in the musical setting.

a way, depict individual personalities in his operas, but he does so always in the solo arias; and even then the result is a compound, a sum total derived from the different affections expressed in a personage's various arias and giving a composite impression comparable to that of an overlaid series of photographs. But not even this much individuality ever appears in ensembles, where the individual is completely swallowed up in the group and becomes for the time being as anonymous as any singer in a chorus. This is true, surprisingly, even in the duets of *Il trionfo dell'onore:* the only exception is the comic duets, where the two personalities are often quite sharply distinguished—not so much by the style of their music as by means of bickering, mockery, and name-calling. It is historically consistent therefore that in the course of the eighteenth century the ensemble of clearly differentiated individuals developed within the comic opera (using the term in the broadest sense) rather than within the *opera seria.*

Il trionfo dell'onore had eighteen performances between 26 November 1718 and 11 January 1719. There is no evidence that it was ever revived either at Naples or elsewhere during Scarlatti's lifetime; at least, no printed librettos are known except the one for Naples. There is a copy of the score in the British Library and another in the Library of Congress which Sonneck (in the library's catalogue of librettos) indicates as "possibly autograph," an inscription which Professor Hanley can validate only to the extent of "copied by a scribe that I believe was close to Scarlatti" (related in a 1969 letter to the author). For performances at Siena in 1940 a score was prepared by Virgilio Mortari,[6] much shortened but adapted with good taste in conformity with the spirit if not the letter of Scarlatti's original.

Scarlatti's last opera for Naples for *Cambise,* performed at San Bartolomeo in February of 1719 with the composer not present. (Presumably he had already left for Rome, where new operas of his were now being presented regularly every season.) Like most of Scarlatti's operas by this time, *Cambise* ran for only a single season at Naples; the only surviving score is a copy preserved in the library of the conservatory at Naples. The plot is an unusually

6. Published by Carisch at Milan in 1941.

extravagant fantasy on actual history. Cambyses was king of Persia from 529 to 522 B.C., between the reigns of Croesus the Great and Darius I. His entire army of 50,000 men is said to have perished in a simoom (a sandstorm) in the course of an expedition of conquest in Egypt. Evidently it was this expedition—in its early and more successful stage—which suggested the background for the opera's plot. According to the libretto (by D. Lalli and S. Biancardi), Cambise had sojourned in Egypt for two years at the court of Rosane, queen of Babylon (a city which, to compound confusion, is occasionally called Memphis). During all this time he was in disguise—perhaps an endurance record for a disguise even in opera plots of this period—and so successful was this little stratagem that both Rosane and her sister Mirena fell in love with the romantic stranger, who called himself Sidaspe. Sidaspe-Cambise himself preferred the sister, and as a convenient means of obtaining her hand in marriage had determined to besiege Babylon-Memphis with his army. Rosane had an ally, Orconte, king of Arabia, who himself was in love with Mirena. After the usual protracted run of misunderstandings, desperate battles, scenes of despairing love, jealousy, suspicion, and general confusion, the couples are finally sorted out: Orconte gets Mirena and Cambise accepts Rosane's generous offer to make him her husband and king of Babylon, which would seem to be an exceptionally appropriate locale for a plot like this.

Now we can be sure that no one, certainly no one in Naples, took this kind of thing seriously; and the proof is the comic scenes, which openly parody and satirize the serious scenes and personages of the opera and in effect spoof them unmercifully. The comic scenes in *Cambise* come at the by now customary places, at the end of each of the first two acts and just before the third act finale; they feature the usual servant couple, a bass and a soprano, and they are unusually long and boisterous. There are of course comic scenes in practically all of Scarlatti's Naples operas, but they are found less often in his operas for Rome. It is conjecturable that the autocratic rulers of Naples, consciously or unconsciously, rather encouraged such scenes in the theatre as a kind of safety valve for the emotions of a turbulent and potentially dangerous populace.

The opening scene of *Cambise* is of a kind that might have been calculated to horrify us today now that we are beginning rather belatedly to have some concern for preserving our natural environment. The description in the libretto of the scene at the beginning of Act I reads:

> A fearful wild forest [*orrida selva*] on the banks of the Nile, along which are seen approaching the mighty Persian warships. From one of these Argivo, the commanding officer, descends, followed by a large number of soldiers. . . . To the sound of military music from the ships, the soldiers cut down all the trees so that the forest becomes a level field; and on this the soldiers prepare redoubts and trenches and other military installations for the security of the encampment. Once these are ready, Cambise and his officers disembark from the leading ship.

To judge from the length of the sinfonia that accompanies this scene, the whole operation takes about three and one-half minutes (though there is a notice in the score that the music may be repeated if necessary). There are two other short incidental sinfonie in *Cambise:* one in Act II, scene 8, to accompany a march before a battle; and another introducing the big final scene at the end of Act III. The instruments for the scene to Act II are two horns, a "*concerto d'oubuoi*" (that is, two parts for oboes and one for bassoons), plus strings and continuo. A notice in the score reads "si può sonare senza l'orchestra se così bisogno," from which we deduce that the word "orchestra" here signifies the strings, lutes, and cembalos in the pit while the wind instruments are perhaps posted on stage. Possibly also in this usage there lurks a reference to the earlier meaning of orchestra as a place rather than a group of instrumentalists. The same meaning is suggested in the autograph score of the prologue to *Telemaco.* It is the horns, oboes, bassoons, and strings that accompany the big aria of Cambise in the first scene of Act I.

On the whole, it must be said that this opera has few arias of real distinction. The accompaniments have some interesting experiments in sonority, but the melodies themselves are too often commonplace, lacking in high points of expressiveness, and without any compelling sense of direction. It may be that Scarlatti was put off by the silly libretto, and if so this would account for the special care he evidently expended on the comic interludes of *Cambise*.

Scarlatti had received a patent of nobility from Pope Clement XI in 1716 and from then on all his title pages bear the title *cavaliere*. In 1718 he obtained another leave of absence from the Viceroy to conduct his new opera *Telemaco* at Rome in the Teatro Capranica, of which his patron Prince Ruspoli was one of the leading promoters. All his remaining known operas were written for Rome: these include *Marco Attilio Regolo* (1719) and *Griselda* (1721); two complete reworkings of operas originally written for Florence in the early 1700s: *Tito Sempronico Gracco* (1702, 1720) and *Turno Aricino* (1704, 1720); and two other operas after *Griselda*, no music of which apparently has survived. It seems clear that by this time Scarlatti felt himself more at ease in the relatively conservative atmosphere of Rome than in Naples, where he was being supplanted in public favor by younger Neapolitans like Domenico Sarro (or Sarri; 1679–1744), Francesco Mancini (1672–1737; Scarlatti's replacement as *maestro di cappella* in 1703–8), and Leonardo Vinci (1690?–1730).

Telemaco is one of Scarlatti's most interesting operas. An idea of the subject matter can be obtained from the *"argumento"* in C. S. Capeci's libretto (Rome, 1718), which reveals with unconscious and rather appealing naivety the way an opera plot would be constructed on the basis of a subject from classical literature:

> The adventures of Telemachus as well as those of his father, Ulysses, are described by Homer in his Odyssey, from which the theme of the present drama has been drawn. To the celebrated author's insufficient narrative we have added that Minerva has destined Telemachus to be the husband of Antiope, daughter of Idomeneus, whom he encounters in the realm of the nymph Calypso, living under the name of Eriphyle, and falls in love with her without knowing who she is. Moreover, Calypso herself has fallen in love with Telemachus, even though her father had already promised her hand in marriage to Adrastus, prince of Corinth. We have also introduced into the opera the personage of Sicoris, son of Atlas, in order to give more scope to the plot, making him to be in love with Antiope by whom he had been made a slave. From all this there

follow the events [*accidenti*] which may be read and seen in the course of the drama.

Another feature of this libretto is the specific listing of machines, as follows: in Act I, (a) Neptune's chariot drawn by tritons and marine monsters; (b) Minerva's chariot on the clouds; and in Act III, (a) ships which are transformed into *mongibelli,* that is, volcanoes; and (b) the gigantic figure (colossus) of Atlas holding up the globe of the heavens, which opens to reveal Minerva and other gods and godesses on their thrones. Also listed are the *balli,* consisting of (a) "furies and demons" at the end of Act I and (b) after Act II, vases of flowers which change into fountains with birds and then into *jardinières* (large flowerpots). Displays and stage effects with machines on such a scale as this one are not common in Scarlatti. He has matched the opening tableau with ceremonial music: introduction for two horns and a "*concerto d'oubouè*" (probably onstage) against full strings with continuo in the "orchestra," followed by an elaborate aria for Neptune (tenor) in the usual da capo form with tempo mark *vivace, e presto* (*vivace* for the general character and mood, *presto* for the speed: a typical kind of distinction in Scarlatti's markings). Then comes a *recitativo stromentato* (arpeggio string chords) in which Neptune announces his determination, in spite of Jove's commands, to oppose the son Telemachus as he has already opposed the father Odysseus. Minerva arrives in her chariot, singing an aria with accompaniment of four-part strings and trumpet onstage alternating and combining with the usual strings and continuo of the "orchestra." In a simple recitative the two deities become reconciled: they then sing a duet "Torni dunque il Ciel sereno," to accompaniment by three separate groups of instruments: one ensemble of two horns, two oboes, and bassoon, on stage; one string ensemble (two violins, viola, violoncello), also onstage; and the usual strings with basso continuo in the "orchestra." It makes a fifteen-staff score, which (as far as I know) is something unique in Scarlatti's operas.

Marco Attilio Regolo, on a libretto attributed to Matteo Noris, is duly listed on the title page of the autograph score (now in the British Library) as "opera 112." It was performed in the Teatro Capranica at Rome during the Carnival season of 1719. By comparison with its predecessors, especially *Telemaco* and *Tigrane, At-*

tilio Regolo gives the impression of a conservative work, a classical example of the late Scarlatti style. The story itself, of course, is classical in the sense that, like so many operas of the late seventeenth and the eighteenth centuries, it is based on an episode from Roman history—this time, of the period of the First Punic War (middle of the third century b.c.). In particular, it celebrates the probity and self-sacrificing heroism of the consul Marcus Attilius Regulus whom later authors, particularly Horace and Cicero, were wont to hold up as an example of the ideal "noble Roman." Typically for an early-eighteenth-century opera libretto, the story of Attilio is combined with other historical or quasi-historical incidents in order to make up the necessary number of lover-pairs and ensure a happy ending, complete with the usual displays of magnanimity.[7] Likewise according to common practice are the use of disguise, a debarkation scene, a pastoral scene in which one character goes to sleep (a man this time), and the comic scenes. These last, for bass and contralto, are unusually long and numerous: there are two in each of the first and third acts and one in Act II. Typically, they come either at the end of an act or just before a *mutazione* (change of stage set). Having only the most tenuous connection with the main plot, more clearly than ever they take on the character of intermezzi, easily detachable, if desired, from the rest of the opera. When *Attilio Regolo* was revived at Bologna in 1724 these comic scenes were perhaps omitted—at any rate there is no trace of them in the Bologna libretto—though it may be that they or some scenes like them were performed between the acts; if so, this would mark a further stage in the evolution of this particular genre of comic opera in the early eighteenth century. There were the customary numerous changes and substitutions of arias at Bologna, thus justifying the notice in the libretto that "la musica è del Sig. Cavaliere Alessandro Scarlatti, ed altri virtuosi."

By comparison with *Telemaco* and the late Neapolitan operas, the score of *Marco Attilio Regolo* is (as has been said) notably con-

7. This is in contrast to the more famous *Attilio Regolo* libretto of Metastasio, set to music by both Hasse and Jommelli (1750 and 1753 respectively), which has no comic scenes and—unusually for this author—has a tragic ending, with a long farewell scene in *recitativo obbligato*.

servative. Except for the perfunctory choral finale at the end of the third act and the one very short debarkation scene, the only important stage display is a scene at the beginning of Act I—almost like a continuation of the overture—consisting of choruses and dances "of the young Carthaginians" accompanied by the full orchestra together with a "strepito di zampogne, e snarccari, e sistri, all'era di barbare nazioni" ("a racket of bagpipes, castanets and sistrums in the manner of barbarous nations"—probably onstage). This is perhaps Scarlatti's extreme effort toward realistic local color in his operas. Otherwise, *Attilio Regolo* consists of an almost unbroken succession of recitatives and arias, plus duets, one trio, and one quartet, the accompaniments being mostly for full string orchestra and continuo. The orchestral sonority in these numbers is exceptionally full since the first violins, instead of virtually doubling the voice as had been Scarlatti's usual practice, now as a rule have their own melodic line enriching the total texture. The *recitativi stromentati*—particularly Fausta's great lamentation over the supposed tomb of Attilio in Act III, scene 9[8]—are especially noteworthy. One other exceptional feature of this opera is the presence of no fewer than eight "interrupted arias," that is, arias that are left incomplete—broken off by recitative either abruptly soon after the beginning or else at the end of part A, involving the omission of the usual part B and of course the usual da capo. Such a procedure would not attract any special attention from a modern audience, but one must remember that listeners in Scarlatti's time were thoroughly conditioned to expect that any aria once begun would continue through its normal course with a contrasting second part, a da capo, and a formal ending. The interruption of an aria therefore, whether comic or serious, being unexpected, would have had a much more noticeable dramatic impact in 1719 than we can easily imagine today.

Carl Reginald Morey has drawn attention to a most unusual aspect of Scarlatti's practice involving the operas of the years 1718–19:[9] it seems that in *Telemaco, Cambise,* and *Attilio Regolo*

8. Alessandro Scarlatti, *Marco Attilio Regolo,* ed. Jocelyn Godwin (Cambridge: Harvard University Press, 1975), pp. 203–6.
9. Morey, "Late Operas of Scarlatti," p. 129.

there are no fewer than seven instances of the same aria appearing in two of the three different operas—sometimes identical in both music and words, sometimes with very slight changes of either words or music or both. In all but one of these translations Scarlatti was taking over music from Naples to use at Rome; in the remaining case, an aria from *Telemaco* served again in *Attilio Regolo*. So far as anyone apparently knows in the present primitive state of Scarlatti research, these are the only times he ever transferred arias bodily from one opera to another, though of course the practice in general was not uncommon in this period. It would not be surprising if similar discoveries were to be made within the corpus of Scarlatti's operas, especially perhaps among those written during that crowded decade of the 1690s at Naples.

Except for the two lost Roman operas of 1721 and 1722 and four arias in a pasticcio at Naples in 1724, Scarlatti's last opera was *Griselda,* which was presumably first staged at the Teatro Capranica in January of 1721. Presumably, since 1721 is the date in the printed libretto and on the title page of the autograph score, of which Acts I and III are in the British Library; but there is ample evidence in the autograph as well as in the libretto of an earlier version (perhaps privately performed in December 1720) which seems to have been hastily altered at the last moment—indeed, after the libretto was printed. The changes are quite extensive: at least 128 lines of recitative and five or six of the original arias were either cancelled or replaced in the revised version, a quartet was added in Act III, and numerous small alterations were made in the recitatives. The explanation of most of these changes is obvious and moreover is one that well illustrates the conditions under which an opera composer worked at that time: Carestini, a new and promising young castrato singer, who evidently had a powerful patron at Rome (possibly Prince Ruspoli himself), had been engaged to make his debut in *Griselda* at the Teatro Capranica in January, in the role of Costanza; for his benefit certainly at least one and probably three new arias were inserted, these additions being balanced by the deletion of one aria each for four of the other singers; moreover, two of Costanza's original arias were completely rewritten with the addition of coloratura passages calculated to show off the debutant star to the best advantage. On the whole, Carestini came out very well in the revisions; what his colleagues in the cast may have thought about them we can only surmise.

The figure of "patient Griselda" had appeared frequently in literature from the time when Boccaccio introduced her in the last tale of his *Decamerone* until Apostolo Zeno chose it as the subject of a libretto which was set to music by Antonio Pollarolo for Venice in 1701. There were at least thirteen other Griselda operas before Scarlatti's, all taking the customary liberties with Zeno's text, introducing changes of locale, additional comic characters, and so on. Zeno's original comic servant was completely omitted in Scarlatti's libretto (although there are a couple of vestigial references to him). As to Griselda herself, that signally unliberated woman and obedient wife, perhaps our contemporary viewpoint was anticipated by Chaucer some 600 years ago:

> Grisild is deed, and eek hir pacience,
> And bothe at oonce buried in Italye;
> For which I crie in open audience,
> No weddid man so hardy be to assayle
> His wyves pacience, in hope to fynde
> Grisilides, for in certain he schal fayle.[10]

Griselda is one of the least spectacular of Scarlatti's operas. The role of the villain Ottone and many scenes between the young lovers Roberto and Costanza, while necessary by convention, are irrelevant to the main line of action, which is the ordeal and eventual triumph of Griselda. But the theme of triumph through patience is not one that is likely to call for startling incidents along the way, and consequently we find that the score as a whole is marked by an atmosphere of uniformity and repose. There is plenty of variety in the score, but it is variety inherent in the musical substance, not dependent on external factors. There is little of the scenic display that is so prominent in *Telemaco* and nothing of the melodramatic horrors of *Mitridate* and *Tigrane*. There are no comic scenes and the three brief choruses are negligible. The real climax of the opera, both dramatically and musically, is Griselda's wonderful accompanied recitative in the last scene of Act III. All

10. Chaucer, "The Clerke's Tale": L'Envoye, 1–6.

Scene from Act III of *Griselda*,
University of California, Berkeley, production, 1976.
PHOTO BY KARL SAARNI.

but five of the preceding thirty-seven scenes are constructed on the conventional pattern of recitative plus da capo aria (or recitative only). There are three duets, one trio, and one quartet, all likewise in da capo form. Most of the accompaniments are for the full string orchestra with continuo; in a few of the arias oboes with independent parts are added to the strings, and the arias in the pastoral scenes in Act III characteristically have independent flute parts with the strings. As in *Attilio Regolo,* Scarlatti's older practice of virtually doubling the voice part by the first violins is now almost totally abandoned in favor of independent first violin parts. Moreover, compared to the earlier operas there is in *Griselda* a noticeable increase of rhythmic independence among the accompanying instruments, producing an unobtrusive contrapuntal texture of more interest and variety than the mere enumeration of the instrumental forces would suggest.

·VI·

The Forms of a Scarlatti Opera:
Scarlatti's Musical Style

THIS LAST CHAPTER will be, in a sense, a da capo of Chapter I
with nonimprovised variations. For the present purpose we shall
concentrate on *Tigrane*, which is one of the best and was certainly
the most successful of the late operas and can therefore appropriately serve to illustrate Scarlatti's typical procedures—
understanding by typical that which exemplifies the normal or
regular features of a certain dramatic and musical style at its
highest point of development. We omit the customary plot synop-
sis, since the story of *Tigrane* is in all essentials like that of Scarlatti's other *drammi per musica* and provides similar occasions for varied musical affections and scenic displays.

How can we describe the musical form of *Tigrane?*

We are sometimes told that the basic musical unit of such an
opera is the aria. This is not true. The basic musical unit is the
recitative-plus-aria, the recitative-aria couple. The common error
on this point arises from regarding the recitative as musically negligible, a mere interpolation due to dramatic necessity, having no
other purpose than to get through as many words as possible in
the shortest possible time and so to prepare the way for the aria to
come. Now it is quite likely that some eighteenth-century composers, and even Scarlatti himself at times, did write recitatives that
sound as if this were their sole object; but Scarlatti's recitatives on
the whole, and at their best, are far from lacking in musical
interest—bearing in mind of course that lyrical melodic lines, balanced repetition and variation of phrases, contrapuntal texture,
and a conventional overall harmonic structure were resources

excluded from recitative by its very nature. What remained therefore was, first, *accuracy of declamation* in the melodic line, which
could be notated in some detail by the rhythm and contour of the
phrase and which an alert singer could modify in both respects in
the direction of even greater accuracy and realism; and second,
the *resources of harmony,* in the progression of a phrase or passage
toward its conventional cadence, in rapid harmonic changes for
highly charged emotional passages, and in the use of particular
tonalities (for example, E minor or the more remote flat and
sharp keys) or of particular chords (such as the diminished
seventh or the Neapolitan sixth) for especially poignant emotional
effects.

More particularly with regard to the conception of the
recitative-plus-aria as the basic musical unit in these operas: the
obvious musical contrast between these two elements, as we have
already noted, is that which generates the constant succession
recitative-aria-recitative-aria throughout an entire act—a con-
tinual contrast, on the one hand, of singing in rapid phrases of
irregular length and irregular melodic outline (depending on the
text, which is sometimes in prose), with stylized though more or
less realistic declamation and no repetition of the words, with accompaniment of the continuo only; and, on the other hand, a sustained melody in balanced (though never mechanically equal)
segments, constant repetition of phrases or single words in the
text (which is always in verse), and accompaniment by an unchanging group of orchestral instruments, the whole organized in
the conventional form

I. Part A: $R_1 V^1 R_2 V^2 R_3$ $(V^3 R_4)$

II. Part B: $R_1 V^1 R_2 V^2$ (R_3)

III. Part A da capo

(R = Ritornello, V = voice)

The contrast, in terms of music, is as great as could well be
imagined. In what, then, does the unity consist? In the first place,
the unity is psychological. The words of the recitative develop a
situation, furnish a stimulus to which the words of the following
aria are a response; in the old phrase, "the recitative loads the
gun, the aria fires it." Corresponding to this distinction, the jag-
ged, irregular phrases of the recitative and its multi-directional

harmonic progressions create an unstable musical situation to which the aria with its continuous melody and broadly organized tonal pattern is the necessary response and resolution. The critical point in this coupling is the harmonic progression from the last chord of the recitative to the first chord of the succeeding aria. In *Tigrane*, as also in Scarlatti's other operas from 1700 on, that is—in proportion of about five cases out of six—a progression from dominant (or mediant, which serves as the dominant surrogate) to tonic. Actually, it is a double-dominant progression, since the last two chords of the recitative always progress from a dominant to a tonic which in turn becomes the dominant of the following aria. The exact figures for *Tigrane* are as follows:

> Total number of arias: 50 (18, 16, 16)
>   in major keys: 36   in minor keys: 14
> Entrance through V
>   to major keys: 19   to minor keys: 11
> Entrance through iii (dominant surrogate)
>   to major keys: 15   to minor keys: 2
> Total entrances through V or iii:
>   arias in major: 34/36   arias in minor: 13/14
> Other entrances: submediant, 2 (to major keys)
>   tonic, 1 (to minor key)

The dominant-tonic connection between a recitative and its aria is also consistently present in Scarlatti's *La caduta de' decemviri* (1697), and somewhat less consistently—in proportion roughly of 2:3—in *Pirro e Demetrio* (1694) and *Rosmene* (1686). It is not at all prominent in Pasquini's *Lisimaco* (1681); it occurs frequently, though not exclusively, in the late operas of Stradella.[1] Leonardo Vinci in his *Artaserse* (1730) prefers rather to end a recitative on the tonic of the following aria—equivalent to an elision of the recitative ending and the aria beginning. In Hasse's *Arminio* (1745, revised 1753) the practice is more often that of Scarlatti, who is said to have been one of Hasse's first teachers: nineteen of the twenty-six recitatives in his *Arminio*, for example, end on the dominant of the following aria.

1. Carolyn Gianturco, "Caratteri stilistici delle opere teatrali di Stradella," *Rivista italiana di musicologia* 6 (1971): 238.

This prevalent dominant-tonic progression from recitative to aria in Scarlatti is a symbol of the essential couple relationship which constitutes the recitative-aria as the basic musical unit of his operas.

Two subsidiary questions relating to this point can be briefly disposed of. What of the case where there are two or more recitatives in succession? In effect, such recitatives can be regarded as a single musical entity. As a rule, the only thing that happens between them is that one character has entered or left the stage, thereby creating what is technically a new scene, with a resulting new number for the second recitative in the finished edition of the score; musically, however, the difference between two successive recitatives and a single long recitative is usually negligible. The essential point is the transition from the last recitative to the next aria.

The other possible question is this: what about the musical relationship between the end of an aria and the beginning of the next recitative? The answer is twofold: (1) the end of an aria marks a break in the musical continuity. The singer leaves the stage; he may even be recalled once or twice for applause, but in any event there is a definite pause before the next scene—and therefore usually the next recitative—begins. (2) As a matter of fact, Scarlatti in *Tigrane* and his other late operas often begins a recitative on the first inversion of the tonic chord of the preceding aria—a gesture toward unification, perhaps—but this chord at once melts into the next one and the shifting modulations of the recitative soon erase any lingering recollection of a tonal connection with the preceding aria. In fact a new musical unit, a new recitative-aria couple has begun.

The forms of the aria in Scarlatti may be illustrated from two examples in *Tigrane:*

I. Aria (Tigrane, soprano) "Il fiero aspetto" in Act III, Scene 11

A	Il fiero aspetto	a	5	The fierce aspect
	d'orrenda morte	b	5	of horrid death
	con *petto forte*	b	5	I will meet with
	incontrerò.	c	4	*courage.*

B	E sol sento io	d	5	I feel only that
	che il cor mi svena	e	5	my heart faints
	l'*acerba pena*	e	5	within me
	che l'idol mio	d	5	with *bitter pain*
	lasciar dovrò.	c	4	because I must
				leave my beloved.

(images italicized)

This is the last aria in this scene, and the last one before a change of set—a normal place for an important "big" aria. "Il fiero aspetto" (see example 5) consists of 103 measures (counting the da capo) with tempo indication *andante e staccato,* metre 3/4, key E-flat major (not a common key in Scarlatti) with part B modulating from B-flat major to F minor and cadencing in G minor as preparation for the return of E-flat major for the da capo. The accompaniment is for full string orchestra with continuo; during the singing the continuo line is, as usual, notated in the tenor clef, unfigured and consistently doubled by the violas or second violins. The prevailing texture of the accompaniment, one often favored by Scarlatti for arias of a solemn nature, is of steadily repeated chords; these are in rhythm of eighth notes in part A and of quarter notes in part B—though the uniformity is interrupted in the second section of part A by recurrence of a dotted-note figure which had been first heard in the orchestral introduction.

Outline of the Form:

PART A

Ritornello I, 9 measures (3 + 4 + 2): strong emphasis on the primary triads of E-flat.

Motives:
1. mm. 1–2
2. m. 3
3. (descending tonic chord-outline) mm. 4–5
   Motives 2–1, mm. 6–7 to preliminary
      cadence on tonic in first inversion
   Motives 2–1, mm. 8–9 to definitive
      cadence on tonic.

Voice I,   mm. 10–17 (4–5): conflation of motives 2 and 3 to cadence on B-flat; emphasis, by wide leaps and long notes, on *morte, forte.*

Ritornello II,   mm. 17–20: chiefly on motive 2, confirming cadence on B-flat and linking to:

Voice II,   mm. 21 (with upbeat)–36. (a) motive 2, sequential through subdominant to half-cadence in E-flat at m. 24; the second member of the sequence is extended upward through one beat and recalls the outline of mm. 6–7 of Ritornello I. (b) mm. 25–31: coloratura passage in triplets, rising sequence to reiteration of motive 1 at m. 29; deceptive cadence, mm. 30–31. (c) mm 32–36: sustained B-flat and octave drop (climax of Voice II): pause for cadenza; mm. 35–36, final cadence to E-flat (tonic) with combination of motives 1 and 2.

Ritornello III,   mm. 36–44 (2+3+2+2): motives 1, 2, and 3; cadence (after a 7-measure period) on tonic first inversion at m. 42, final cadence at m. 44.

PART B

Voice III,   mm. 45–63. Part I: 2+2+2, 3+2 measures, to F minor; Part II: 4 (to G minor) 4, with pause and extended final cadence. Allusions to motif 3. D^7 on "pena" and in last phrase (= V of V), with melisma on "lasciar."

(Ritornello IV, Ritornello I)

II. Aria (Policare, alto) "Chi mi dice spera, spera" in III, 14

A	Chi mi dice spera, spera?	a	8
	Spera un *eco* mi risponde	b	8
	E quel onde *mormorando*	c	8
	Par che temprino il mio duolo.	d	8
	E cantando il rossignuolo	d	8
	Pur accresce il mio sperar.	e	7
B	E da un eco lusinghiera	a	8
	Da un vezzoso *rusceletto*	f	8
	E da un musico augeletto	f	8
	Trova pace il mio penar.	e	7

100

Who says to me, "Hope, hope"?
"Hope," an echo answers me,
And this murmuring wave
Seems to temper my sorrow

And the nightingale with his singing
Increases my hope.

And from a flattering echo,
From a charming brooklet,
And from a singing bird
    My suffering finds peace.

This too is the last aria in a scene; what follows is a comic scene, which is psychologically equivalent to a change of stage set and therefore calls for an immediately preceding aria of rather large dimensions. "Chi mi dice spera, spera" (see example 6) has sixty-five measures (again counting the da capo) in tempo *andante moderato*, 4/4, E minor with part B modulating from G major through A minor to a cadence on B (dominant preparation for return of part A). The accompaniment is for the normal string orchestra, supplemented by a vocal "eco" and a nightingale (these presumably offstage): the continuo is notated as in the previous example, though with a rather large proportion of the phrases in part A being accompanied by the full strings with the bass figured. As the "image" words of the text, "mormorando," and "rus-celetto," suggest, the accompaniment features a steady smooth undulation of sixteenth notes with second violins and violas, which ceases only toward the end of part B with the words "pace" and "penar." The vocal line, doubled throughout by the first violins, is similar to those of the orchestra, though less continuously ornate. The whole very much resembles Meroe's "Sussurando il venticello" which comes only two scenes earlier, but the one intervening aria is of quite different character, so the well-known later eighteenth-century rule against two arias of the same type coming in immediate succession is observed. Still, all three of the arias here in question are in minor keys, a local preponderance of the minor mode which is exceptional in late Scarlatti. It is particularly exceptional in this opera, for the majority of the arias in *Tigrane* are in major keys and in fast tempo.

Especially notable in this aria is the way in which Scarlatti has so sensitively captured the mood of alternating despair and hope, with despair ultimately prevailing. The preceding recitative ends in B minor with Policare's words:

> Bella speranza mia:
> Deh! deh! mensognera
> Non esser sempre a un che spera.

The last word "spera" is sung on the normal recitative closing cadence of the descending fourth B–F-sharp, with the usual dominant chord below it in the continuo; at the resolution to the tonic B-minor chord, which ordinarily of course would be sounded in the continuo only, there is a sudden intervention from the offstage "eco," repeating the word "spera" on the same two notes of the descending fourth. Immediately comes the aria: "Segue l'aria. *Attaca subito*"—a rare direction in Scarlatti. Policare begins on a single, startled, isolated unaccompanied note B with the word "Chi?"—a little touch of realism; and of course his B immediately becomes the dominant of his E-minor aria, to be heard unambiguously as such at the da capo.[2]

The form of this aria is somewhat unusual. The first three measures are in effect a transition from the recitative, with continuous reiterated tiny echoes on the word "spera." The aria properly gets under way only at measure 4, starting out quite cheerfully in G major, always with the little echoes on "spera"; but by the time we get to "duolo" we are in A minor (the subdominant instead of the usual dominant), with a flatted second in the preliminary cadence at measure 14. The second part of the A section (during which the nightingale sings) is in E minor, ending with mournful roulades and cadencing with a lowered second, on "sperar"—a deliberate contradiction of the word, symbolizing the really felt hopelessness of the "spera" commands. Here, just before the final cadence, occurs the usual pause for an "improvised" cadenza. Part B begins more cheerfully in G major, but soon goes

2. This passage ought to serve as an argument for those who believe that the normal way of performing a recitative cadence in Scarlatti is with the penultimate dominant chord sounding simultaneously with the descending fourth in the voice instead of after it, as evidently became the practice later in the eighteenth century.

into the minor mode again—strangely enough, on the word "pace"—which is followed by the same laboring chromatic twists as before, but now more intense, on "penar"; all this comes once in A minor and again in B minor. Then of course follows the da capo. In view of the prevalent steadily running sixteenth notes it is difficult to imagine how a singer would have ornamented this aria, except perhaps with short trills or appoggiaturas at the cadences, possibly slow trills or turns on the few long notes, but of course with complete freedom at the cadenza.

With these examples as foreground let us now summarize and generalize the characteristics of Scarlatti's arias as revealed specifically in *Tigrane* but as applicable generally to his other operas, especially those of the period 1700–1721.

1. The texture is contrapuntal: not the imitative counterpoint of the fugue, but rather that of the solo concerto, consisting of a tune and a bass with melodically related moving inner voices whose function is primarily rhythmic.

2. The form is like that of the solo concerto, with alternating tutti and solo sections, the whole subsumed under the A B A structure of the da capo aria.

3. Thematically, part B is related to part A in a manner analogous to the text relation of the two parts: sometimes as contrast but more typically as continuation or commentary. The material of part B is never conceived as a second theme in the sense of some sonata-form movements of the later eighteenth century.

4. The dominating motive or musical subject of an aria always gives the impression of having sprung at once and irresistibly out of the specific sense, feelings, and images of the text. It seems that, as Scarlatti hinted in his letter to Prince Ferdinand, when he read the words there occurred at once something like an inaudible click in his mind, and there was the right musical idea all ready to be written down. Not all vocal music, no matter how beautifully it fits the text, gives so irresistibly this impression of instant, spontaneous generation of the music out of the words. (Perhaps Mozart is the composer most nearly like Scarlatti in this respect.)

5. The initial motive-complex is developed in continuous motoric rhythm, in which the voice and all the instruments par-

ticipate contrapuntally—but not equally, since the voice always predominates. The voice may at times hold one note against continuous movement in the orchestral parts. Rhythmic continuity will be interrupted only for exceptional, specific dramatic reasons, or for the conventional slowdown at the end of part B, or for the free cadenza near the end of part A of the aria.

6. The initial phrase clearly defines the tonality of the aria. There is never any tonal ambiguity, but the boundaries of a given key seem to be wider in Scarlatti than in our conventional harmony textbooks: F major, for example, admits an E-flat or a B-natural, depending on the direction of movement of the individual lines. The opening ritornello will cadence in the tonic without having modulated. The first voice section cadences in the dominant in a major aria, or in the relative major or dominant minor if the aria is in a minor key. The second ritornello, unless extremely short, is apt to start out again in the tonic and then lead quickly to one of the nearly related keys, whence the second voice section takes over with wider-ranging modulations (usually in the subdominant direction), frequently a more or less extended coloratura passage, and with a definitive return to the tonic at the end. The tonic here will be strongly defined at the last cadence and additionally confirmed by a preceding pause and an improvised vocal cadenza. The third ritornello is apt to be a shortened version of the first. Part B of the aria is usually thinner in texture and often marked by a general slowing down of the rhythm, together with more remote modulations away from the principal key, possibly going into a short coloratura passage and modulating at the end (sometimes, it seems, rather hurriedly) to a cadence on the conventional secondary tonal center—in a major aria, the mediant minor or the dominant, and in a minor aria as a rule the dominant minor. Here the fourth ritornello may be simply a da capo repetition of the first or, less often, a shortened version of the same with a dal segno back to the beginning of the first voice section of part A.

7. Within any given section of an aria, but especially in the second section of part A and the latter portion of part B, a characteristic procedure is the continuation of a motive in sequential form—usually a tonal rather than a modulating sequence, the

melodic unit being typically two half-measures over a barline. Again typically, all the lines in the texture will be involved in such a sequence.

8. The harmonic rhythm in Scarlatti's arias is fairly fast. Often it seems faster than it is because of the way in which he varies the harmonic durations within a period. There is nothing resembling a regular pendulumlike change of chord at the first beat, or the first and third beats, of each measure; moreover, changes hardly ever occur at the same rate in two successive measures. Normally, of course, the harmonic rhythm accelerates during the approach to a cadence, but there will often be places earlier in the phrase where the contrapuntal movement of the bass produces a change of harmony on some of the single beats or even half-beats of the measure, with the incidental consequence that some notes in the melody that look (for example) like passing tones turn out to be harmonic tones. The irregularity together with the comparatively fast rate of harmonic change is one feature that distinguishes Scarlatti's musical style from that of later eighteenth-century composers—though there are signs, in some of the Roman operas after 1718, that he was beginning to be influenced (no doubt unconsciously) in this respect by the practice of his younger contemporaries.

9. Finally, the phrasing in a Scarlatti aria is generally irregular, in the sense that many phrases do not consist of two or a multiple of two measures and that practically all the next-larger formal units either consist of an odd number of measures or else contain so many odd-measured subunits that no impression of regular periodicity results. This irregularity—this variety, or flexibility— of phrasing, in connection with the unchanging persistence of the same time signature and tempo throughout an aria, results in a certain sense of something always unexpected, unpredictable, within an overruling frame of regularity.[3]

So much for the common features of the individual arias with their recitatives. Now what of the order of arrangement of these units within the larger unit of the single act? Here we must take account of extramusical factors. Both librettist and composer

3. See also Luigi Ronga, "Motivi critici su Alessandro Scarlatti," *Rivista musicale italiana* 56 (1954): 137.

knew well that to avoid monotony—the one unforgivable sin in the theatre—they must not have too many arias of the same kind too close together; in practice, the rule seems to have been that no aria should ever be immediately followed by another aria of the same kind. But if all the arias conformed to the model we have just described, in what could a difference of "kind" consist? First of all, of course, in the text, which in accord with the action of the drama would express different ideas and sentiments, with a limited range of differences in the metre and form of the poetry. These differences could be reflected in the music by differences, not of the overall form, but of the range, timbre, and quality of the singer's voice and more generally of tempo, metre, tonality, and orchestral accompaniment. Taking for example only the succession of tonalities in the arias and ensembles of *Tigrane* we find the following order:

ACT I

D-D-C-A-G-F-A-E♭ || B♭-D-a-D-E-g || *D-B♭-A-G*

ACT II

A-B♭-F || g-C-f || c-D-e-A || B♭-b-c-F || *F-C-d-G*

ACT III

d-a-E-c-B♭-A || d-a-E♭ || *d-g-e-F-D-G* || G-D

capitals: major keys
lowercase: minor keys
italics: comic scenes
|| : change of stage set

Of course it would be possible—human ingenuity in such matters apparently knowing no limits—to deduce from the above some kind of imaginary overall tonal plan, for example: Act I in D major, Act II in the subdominant region, Act III returning to D major; possible, but irrelevant, not to say arbitrary. (For example, the first and last scenes are festive, festivity means trumpets, and trumpets are in D.) What certainly does emerge is the care to avoid tonal monotony; and even this result is largely incidental to another factor, namely the association of certain tonalities with certain moods or ranges of feeling which seems to have been rather widely accepted by theorists and composers of the eighteenth century.[4]

Less important in the general musical form, but far more important in the practical business of the theatre, was the number, kinds, and distribution of arias assigned to each of the individual singers. There was a definite "pecking order": the more important you were, both in the plot and in your reputation, the more arias you would have. The distribution in the Naples production of *Tigrane* (and this is typical for Scarlatti's late operas) was as follows:

Tigrane (soprano castrato) 10 arias and 1 fragment of an aria
Tomiri (soprano) 7 arias and 2 fragments, 2 duets
Policare (alto) 7 arias, 2 duets
Moroe (soprano) 7 arias and 1 fragment, 1 duet
Doraspe (tenor) 4 arias, 1 duet
Oronte (soprano castrato) 1 aria and 1 fragment
Dorilla (comic alto) 2 arias, 4 duets
Orcone (comic bass) 2 arias, 4 duets

In addition to scenes so far considered there are others of a special nature in Scarlatti's operas. Among these are what may be called spectacular scenes—which involve brilliant décor, a crowded stage, and a full orchestra with oboes, bassoons, trumpets, and (from *Tigrane* onwards) horns. Such scenes may also include processions and ballets, with choruses or ensembles. As a rule, an opera will open with a scene of this kind and will close with a similar though less extensive display at the end of Act III, thus making a kind of frame within which the action of the opera takes place. Equally regular in the form of a Scarlatti opera are the pastoral scenes (usually with flutes in the orchestra), which come at or near the beginning of the second act. Other kinds of special scenes—debarkations, spectres, incantations, episodes involving *recitativo stromentato,* and so on—occur in most of Scarlatti's operas, but their placing is always variable and they have no such regular function in the formal order as the pastoral scenes seem to have.

More important in the form, however, are the comic scenes

4. See lists and references in Claude Crussard, "Marc-Antoine Charpentier theoricien," *Revue de musicologie* 27 (1945): 63–66.

which, as we know, regularly come at the end of each of the first two acts and just before the final scene of Act III. These comic scenes had always only a tenuous connection with the main plot, symbolized by the occasional appearance of the two comic personages in the serious scenes and sometimes also by having them indulge in outright parody or travesty of serious elements in the main action. Both kinds of connection are present in the comic scenes of *Tigrane*. For one example: there are three deadly serious episodes in the first act that involve *recitativo stromentato;* at the start of the comic interlude which closes this act Orcone (bass) has been pretending to be a magician, and challenged by his partner Dorilla to give a demonstration, he reluctantly proceeds to do so, stammering all the while from fright lest he be successful. His conjuration, in recitative, is accompanied by full orchestra. Dorilla herself then goes through a similar routine, likewise with a passage of *recitativo stromentato*. (The rest of this comic interlude is more conventional, while the corresponding scenes in Acts II and III rely largely on the device of chattering in Bolognese dialect or in a species of German and Latin.) Apart from the texts, however, the formal importance of the comic scenes in Scarlatti's operas depends on a clearly marked contrast between the musical style of those scenes and that of the rest of the opera: (1) Only in the comic scenes do we hear a bass voice.[5] (2) The orchestra in the comic scenes is limited typically to a single line for violins *unisoni* over the continuo. (3) The tempo is practically always a fast allegro. (4) The vocal line is set syllabically; seldom does a single syllable have more than one or two notes and there is no coloratura unless for parody. (5) The melodic line moves by leap more often than by step. (6) Minor keys generally are avoided, as are also the more remote major keys of A, E, and E flat; many arias and duets will be in the "neutral" key of F major.

These comic scenes in Scarlatti, being musically as well as dramatically set off from the rest of the opera, have a distinctive function in the overall form of the work. Not only do the first two comic intermezzi mark the ends of Acts I and II, but also the third

5. An exception in the late operas is the role of Mitridate in *Ciro;* but it is a small part in the plot and this Mitridate is nothing but a shepherd, whose social position is at least as low as that of a servant.

one, as far as the musical structure is concerned, marks virtually the end of Act III. What follows this last comic scene is, to be sure, the dénouement of the drama; but from the musical viewpoint this is less significant, consisting as it usually does only of recitatives and the very brief, rather perfunctory closing ensemble to celebrate the *lieto fine*. There is—exceptionally—in *Tigrane* one big aria in this final scene; but it is dramatically superfluous and musically not up to Scarlatti's usual standard. One gets the impression that it was inserted only at the insistence of the singer, the celebrated castrato soprano Nicolini.[6] If this was the case, it is typical of the conditions under which opera librettists and composers had to work at this time.

6. Probably Nicolò Grimaldi (1673–1732) who had sung in the premiére of Scarlatti's *Caduta de' decemviri* at Naples in 1697, and also in *Pirro e Demetrio* at London in 1708 and in Handel's *Rinaldo* in 1711. He later became director of the Teatro San Bartolomeo and supervised the production of Scarlatti's *Cambise* in 1719.

EPILOGUE:

A Brief History
of Scarlatti's Reputation

As SCARLATTI by the time of his death had practically vanished from the ken of musicians and writers on music, we find few references to him in later literature of the eighteenth and nineteenth centuries. Raguenet in 1702 had called Scarlatti "a prodigy of music" and singled out for special praise two arias from *Pirro e Demetrio* ("Veder parmi un ombra nera" and "Germana addio") as "two of the most masterly airs ever composed for the theatre."[1] He also praises Scarlatti's recitative—with particular reference to the cantatas—"where he makes use of all sorts of dissonance to express the force of the words and afterwards resolves 'em so well that indeed the most beautiful concords are hardly so sweet and harmonious as his discords." Raguenet's is one of the very few opinions of Scarlatti's music that seems to be based on having actually heard it. His judgment appeared at a time when Scarlatti was at the height of his fame. But by 1725 with Bonnet-Bourdelot's *Histoire de la musique et de ses effets* we have only Le Cerf de la Viéville's vague reference to "le sublime des Melani & des Scarlati"[2]—a curious coupling, if the reference is to Jacopo Melani who died when Scarlatti was sixteen years old—and a mention of "Scarlati" as among the "derniers Orphées d'Italie" who unlike their countryman "Luigi" (presumably Luigi Rossi,

1. François Raguenet, *Parallèle des italiens et des françois en ce qui regarde la musique* (Paris: J. Moreau, 1702). Modern version of the English translation (1709) in *Musical Quarterly* 32 (1946): 411–36.
2. J. L. Le Cerf de la Viéville, *Comparaison de la musique italienne et de la musique françoise*, vol. 1 (Brussels: F. Foppens, 1704); reprinted in Jacques Bonnet, *Histoire de la musique, et de ses effets*, vol. 2 (Amsterdam: J. Royer, 1725; reprint ed., Graz, 1966), p. 95.

1598–1653) had not "s'étoit formé à Paris" and had therefore, as Italians, regrettably "soigneusement cultivé les defauts de leur nation."[3] Equally patriotic was the anonymous author (L'Abbé Pellegrin?) of a *Dissertation sur la musique françoise et italienne* published at Amsterdam in 1754, who lists Scarlatti among the Italian composers "qui ont fait des airs et des opéras, qui sont dans le goût françoise, par conséquent d'un beau naturel" and commends Scarlatti along with Carissimi and Bononcini for music "d'aussi bon goût que la Françoise dans se pureté." An anonymous and undated "Lettre écrite de l'autre monde,"[4] refers to "Scarlatti, Bononcini avec quelques autres Italiens disciples et imitateurs éternels de Lulli." (Evidently by now we are wholly in the realm of mythology.) Heinichen in *Der Generalbass in der Composition* (1728) refers to the "extravagant," "irregular," and "unnatural" harmonies in Scarlatti's cantatas and chooses one of them (*Lascia, deh lascia al fine di tormentarmi più*) as an advanced, difficult exercise in realizing a bass.

In Dr. John Brown's *Dissertation on the Rise, Union, and Power . . . of Poetry and Music* (London, 1763) we read:

> The *Da capo*, which is so striking an absurdity in the more modern operas, was not used in those of older date. Even Colonna, who lived about the middle of the 16th [*sic*] century, employed it not. . . . But in an Opera of Old Scarlatti (intitled *La Teodora*) composed in 1673 [*recte* 1692], the Da capo is found, though not in all his songs. After that Period, the Use of it seems to have become general: For in an Opera of Gasparini (intitled *Il Tartaro nella Chine*) composed in 1715, the Da capo is found in every song.[5]

This seems to be the first promulgation of what may be called the "Teodora theory" of the origin of the da capo aria, which had a long life in musical literature. Burney refuted it by citing earlier examples of the da capo, but Gerber repeats it in 1814,[6] as do

---

3. Le Cerf de la Viéville, *Comparaison,* vol. 3 (1706); reprinted in Bonnet, vol. 4 (1725; reprint ed., 1966), p. 206.

4. "Par L'A. D. F. à M. F." (Paris, n.d.). The title adds, "par Suard d'après Barbieri." Is this the J.-B. Suard (1733–1817) who was a friend of Grétry?

5. Perhaps the reference is to Gasparini's *Taican, Re della Cine* (Venice, 1707).

6. Ernst Ludwig Gerber, *Neues historisches-biographisches Lexikon der Tonkünstler* (Leipzig: A. Kühnel, 1812–14; reprint ed., Graz, 1966).

likewise Choron and Fayolle in 1817, Stafford in his *History of Music* (1830), and Fétis in the first edition of his *Biographie Universelle* (1837). It was refuted once more in the revised edition (1846) of Kiesewetter's *Geschichte des europäischen-abendländischen . . . Musik,* but pops up again nevertheless in Hermann Mendel's *Musikalisches Conversations-Lexikon* (1878), the standard German musical encyclopaedia of its time. The article by Franz Gehring in the first edition of *Grove's Dictionary* (1883), which is generally critical of earlier biographical information about Scarlatti, refers to *Teodora* but adds as though reluctantly that "instances of it [*sc.* the da capo] do occur before his [Scarlatti's] time," citing Kiesewetter. The first edition of Emil Naumann's *Illustrierte Musikgeschichte* (1885) attributes the invention of the da capo to the Florentine-Roman composer A. F. Tenaglia in his opera *Clearco* (1661?) but adds wistfully that Scarlatti "improved and established" it. All this, however, does not prevent our finding in the English translation of the fourth edition of Lavignac's *Music and Musicians* (New York, 1905) that Scarlatti "created the aria type [*sc.* the da capo] long in use in the Italian school."

I have pursued the "Teodora theory" in some detail because it is a good example of the confusion that always ensues when writers feel obliged to make sweeping statements about a large body of music most of which they have never even seen, much less heard. It is impossible to know how much of the opera music of Scarlatti and his contemporaries was actually available to historians in the eighteenth and nineteenth centuries.[7] Presumably the original scores remained in the possession of the patrons to whom they were dedicated, the copies in the possession of those who had ordered them; and from such sources a limited number of items gradually found their way first into the hands of private collectors

---

7. Evidently not much was available when John Sainsbury compiled his *Dictionary of Musicians,* published at London in 1824 (reprint ed., 1966), 2:417: "Until the time of Scarlatti, the overture to an opera consisted of a meagre obligato symphony, produced by certain routine and frequently in bad taste. Scarlatti reformed this department of the opera, and established it less upon the form than upon the foundation of the work itself, making it a species of musical prologue or programme of the action."

and later—in what manner or through what channels we seldom know—into libraries and other collections open to the public: notably, as far as the operas are concerned, to the British Library in London, the conservatory and national libraries in Paris and Brussels, the famous Santini collection now at Münster, libraries at Dresden and Vienna, and to a multitude of libraries in Italy, especially at Naples, Bologna, and Modena. But most of the early historians seem to have relied on tradition and imagination rather than first-hand knowledge of the sources. A typical example is Algarotti's remark in his *Saggio sopra l'opera in musica* (1755) about the arias: "Old Scarlatti was the first who infused life, movement, and spirit in them. It was he who clothed their nakedness with the splendid attire of noble accompaniments, but they are dealt out by him in a sober and judicious manner. They were by no means intricate or obscure, but open and obvious; highly finished, yet free from all the minuteness of affection"[8]—and so on. The statements of Dr. Burney, who actually saw some of Scarlatti's music on his visit to Italy in 1770, are a refreshing exception to the vagueness of other early historians; as one example: "This abuse of overloaded cadenzas is not of very ancient standing, for in a serious opera of old Scarlatti composed in 1717 there is not one ad libitum to be found."[9]

It is from Dr. Burney that the long-standing identification of Scarlatti as the founder of the "Neapolitan school of opera" took its beginning—possibly due to the fact that so much of Burney's information about Scarlatti came from Hasse, who claimed to have been Scarlatti's pupil. Already in La Borde's *Essai* of 1780 we find Scarlatti identified as "un des plus fameux professeurs de cette école" and are informed that "outre ses ouvrages charmans nous lui devons le fameux Hasse."[10] Gerber echoes this in the first edition of his *Lexicon* (1792) and adds "waren seine [sc. Scarlatti's] Einsichten, Kenntnisse und Erfahrungen die Zuflucht aller

8. From the anonymous English translation, (1768): in Oliver Strunk, *Source Readings in Music History* (New York: W. W. Norton, 1950), p. 667.

9. *The Present State of Music in France and Italy* (London: T. Becket, 2d. ed., 1773), p. 377. The reference is possibly to *Il trionfo dell'onore* of 1718.

10. J.-B. de La Borde, *Essai sur la musique ancienne et moderne* (Paris: E. Onfroy, 1780), 3:235.

jungen Künstler, denen es von gründliche Belehrung zu thun war." By the time we come to W. C. Stafford's *History of Music* Leo, Porpora, Vinci, and Durante have all become members of "Scarlatti's school."[11] Fétis in the second edition of his *Biographie universelle* (1883) adds Logroscino to the list but removes Leo.

Meanwhile the theory of evolution or "progress" was making its way into musical history. According to Kiesewetter Scarlatti was "an individual who desired to assist the art in a still more elevated flight, and by his exertions to prepare it for its future exalted condition," being a composer who was "a century in advance of his time."[12] It is consistent with this idea that the first edition of *Grove's Dictionary* (1883) calls Scarlatti "the creator of modern opera." A more sophisticated version of the evolutionary view appears in Naumann: "After [Scarlatti's] death no one was found capable of maintaining the standard of excellence set up by the fruitful Neapolitan, and it consequently deteriorated and fell away into the merely pleasing, *galant,* and popular operatic. . . . In giving melody the place of honor [Scarlatti] paved the way for that inevitable decline of dramatic truth and musical expression which set in soon after his death." Rolland takes a similar dim view of the later eighteenth-century Italian opera but sees the decline as beginning with Scarlatti himself, after the summit had been attained in the works of his predecessors Stradella and Francesco Provenzale.

Modern Scarlatti scholarship begins (after Eitner's *Quellen-Lexikon*) with Edward J. Dent's *Alessandro Scarlatti,* first published at London in 1905 and reissued with additional notes by Frank Walker in 1960. In many ways, this book is still a most valuable compendium of information about Scarlatti's life and works. It is based on first-hand knowledge of the documents about Scarlatti's life and of the scores themselves, which Dent had studied in the various European libraries, particularly those of Italy. It deals with Scarlatti's works as a whole, not only the operas. It places

---

11. *Constable's Miscellany* (Edinburgh, 1830), 3:205.
12. Raphael Georg Kiesewetter, *Geschichte der europäisch-abendländischen oder unserer heutigen Musik* (Leipzig: Breitkopf & Härtel, 1834, enlarged 2d. ed., 1846; Eng. trans. Robert Müller, London: Newby, 1846, reprint ed., New York, 1973).

Scarlatti within the historical framework of his time, provides generous samples of the music, and is seasoned throughout with critical observations about details of the style—observations that are always stimulating, even (or especially) when one feels impelled to disagree with them.

Twenty-two years elapsed before the publication of the next book dealing with Scarlatti's music, Alfred Lorenz's *Scarlattis Jugendoper* (Augsburg, 1927). This work consists of a detailed technical study of Scarlatti's operas up to *La caduta de' decemviri*, with special reference to the forms and key schemes both in the individual arias and in each opera as a whole. Lorenz applied to Scarlatti the same methods of analysis which had enabled him to discover broad tonal patterns in Wagner's music dramas, with results which most later scholars find in both cases to soar beyond the bounds of legitimate inference from the facts. Lorenz, however, has the merit of having cleared up a great many formerly confused or unclear details about Scarlatti's life and work, and above all to have made available, in the second volume of his book, some 200 musical examples of arias, recitatives, and sinfonias from the early operas—an anthology upon which students even now are almost entirely dependent for first-hand knowledge of Scarlatti's opera music.

The third and most recent published full-scale study is *Alessandro Scarlatti* by Roberto Pagano and Lino Bianchi (Turin, 1972), which not only takes into account the results of all the considerable Scarlatti scholarship of the last fifty years in the shape of numerous monographs, catalogues, and other publications, but also adds a great deal of new information about Scarlatti's early life and presents a penetrating study of the oratorios in particular. A very important feature of this publication is a 278-page general catalogue of all Scarlatti's works compiled by Giancarlo Rostirolla.[13] This catalogue not only is practically exhaustive (as far as our present information goes) but also is so intelligently organized as to make it most convenient for consultation. It gives all the known original sources of Scarlatti's works, lists the eighteenth-

13. A new edition of the catalogue is announced; see also supplement (by Reinhard Strohm) in *Rivista italiana di musicologia* II (1976): 314–23.

century and the modern editions, and concludes with a bibliography of the works from which the information in the catalogue has been derived. Similar bibliographies appended to each chapter of the book give altogether a practically complete listing of the important published scholarly literature on Scarlatti.

APPENDIX:
MUSIC EXAMPLES

1. ARIA: "Spesso il ciel,"
from *La principessa fedele,* ACT I, SCENE 3

2. ARIA: "Quando poi vedrai lo strale," from *La principessa fedele,* ACT I, SCENE 17

vrai pie - tà___ pie - tà___ pie - tà___

___, n'a-vrai pie - tà___, pie - tà, n'a-vrai pie - tà.

Chè sco - prir___, sco-

prir pia-ga mor-ta-le nè sa-nar - la____ è cru-del-tà____, è cru-del-

tà; chè sco-prir pia-ga mor-ta-le nè sa-nar - la____ è cru-del-

tà____, è cru-del - tà____, è cru-del - tà.

6   6 6   **Da capo**

3. ARIA: "Patrii numi,"
from *Mitridate Eupatore*, ACT II, SCENE 1

etc.

4. Aria: "Esci omai," from *Mitridate Eupatore,* ACT III, SCENE 3

mo - re, da que - sta, da que - sto sen, da que -

sto, da que - sto sen.

128

5. ARIA: "Il fiero aspetto,"
from *Tigrane,* ACT III, SCENE 11

te in-con-tre-rò——, in-con-tre - rò;

il fie-ro a-spet - to d'or-ren-da

in-con-tre - rò l'a-spet-to fie - ro, Solo

mor - te con pet-to for - - - - - - -

te, for - te   in-con-tre - rò,   con pet-to for -

te   in-con-tre - rò, in-con-tre - rò.

E sol sen - to io che il cor mi sve - na l'a - cer - ba pe - na

Solo

che l'i - dol mi - o la - sciar__, la-sciar do - vrò,__ l'a - cer - ba pe -

na che __ l'i - dol mio la - sciar, la - sciar_____ do - vrò.

Da capo

6. ARIA: "Chi mi dice spera, spera," from *Tigrane,* ACT III, SCENE 13

Qui si sente il canto del rossignuolo

lo;　　　　　　　　　　　　　　　　　　　　　　　　e can -

tan - do il ros - si - gnuo-lo,　　can - tan-do,　　can - tan-do il ros - si -

gnuo - lo　　pur ac - cre - sce,　　pur ac - cre - sce il mio spe-rar,　　il

Solo

Qui cessa il rossignuolo

E da un

e - co lu - sin - ghie - ra, lu - sin - ghie - ra, da un vez-zo - so ru - scel -

let - to e da un mu - si - ca au-gel - let - to tro-va pa

137

Da capo

138

Index

Design: Wolfgang Lederer
Compositor: Typesetting Services
Printer: Thomson-Shore
Binder: Thomson-Shore
Text: VIP Baskerville
Calligraphy: Wolfgang Lederer.
Cloth: Roxite Vellum C56528 & Roxite Linen C57527
Paper: 55 lb. book A-69

ALESSANDRO SCARLATTI

An Introduction to His Operas

by DONALD JAY GROUT

*A*LESSANDRO SCARLATTI (1659-1725), father of Domenico Scarlatti, has too long stood in the shadow of the four great masters of the eighteenth century, Bach and Handel, and Haydn and Mozart. With this readable introduction to Alessandro Scarlatti's operas, Donald Jay Grout contributes to the revaluation and restoration of Scarlatti's work that he has begun with his complete modern edition of the operas.

Historically, Scarlatti's operas mark the culmination of the first hundred years of Italian opera. Their conventions of stage scenery and costume, of dramatic subject matter, of poetic form and language, and of musical form, though they may seem remote to us today, are perfectly consistent within themselves and perfectly consonant with the social conditions of their time and place. With this book Professor Grout helps make those conventions understandable to today's music-lovers. He discusses Alessandro Scarlatti's life and work in the context of eighteenth-century Naples and Rome, and presents an analysis of the music and librettos of the operas.

This book is based on Professor Grout's Ernest Bloch Lectures, delivered at the University of California, Berkeley, in 1976.